P9-DIY-659

A Gift for

_____

From

_____

A MOTHER'S
Prayers

FOR HER CHILDREN

Nancy Ann Yaeger

BETHANY HOUSE PUBLISHERS
Minneapolis, Minnesota

A Mother's Prayers for Her Children
Copyright © 2005
Nancy Ann Yaeger

Cover and interior design: The DesignWorks Group; cover, David Uttley; interior, Robin Black. www.thedesignworksgroup.com

Unless otherwise identified, Scripture quotations are taken from the HOLY BIBLE, NEW INTERNATIONAL VERSION®. Copyright © 1973, 1978, 1984 by International Bible Society. Used by permission of Zondervan Publishing House. All rights reserved.

Scripture quotations identified NRSV are from the New Revised Standard Version of the Bible, copyright 1989 by the Division of Christian Education of the National Council of Churches of Christ in the U.S.A. Used by permission. All rights reserved.

Scripture quotations identified NCV are from *The Holy Bible, New Century Version*. Copyright © 1987, 1988, 1991 by Word Publishing, Dallas, Texas 75039. Used by permission.

Scripture quotations identified RSV are from the Revised Standard Version of the Bible. Copyright 1946, 1952, 1971 by the Division of Christian Education of the National Council of Churches of Christ in the USA. Used by permission.

Scripture quotations identified NLT are from the *Holy Bible*, New Living Translation, copyright © 1996. Used by permission of Tyndale House Publishers, Inc., Wheaton, Illinois 60189. All rights reserved.

Scripture quotations identified TLB are from *The Living Bible* © 1971 owned by assignment by Illinois Regional Bank N.A. (as trustee). Used by permission of Tyndale House Publishers, Inc., Wheaton, IL 60189. All rights reserved.

All rights reserved. No part of this publication may be reproduced, stored in a retrieval system, or transmitted in any form or by any means—electronic, mechanical, photocopying, recording, or otherwise—without the prior written permission of the publisher and copyright owners.

Published by Bethany House Publishers
11400 Hampshire Avenue South
Bloomington, Minnesota 55438

Bethany House Publishers is a division of
Baker Publishing Group, Grand Rapids, Michigan.

Printed in China

ISBN 0-7642-0140-9

To God
All that [I] have accomplished
you have done for [me].

To Daniel, Allison, and Paul
My children whom I pray for daily
I have no greater joy than to hear that my
children are walking in the truth.

3 JOHN 4

To Mom and Dad
My parents who taught me how to pray
One generation will commend your works to
another; they will tell of your mighty acts.

PSALM 145:4

Contents

Introduction

If you are a mother, you are busy. Many times it may be challenging to utter more than a vague prayer for your children. My own need for focused prayer for my three children prompted the writing of this book.

A Mother's Prayers for Her Children equips you with 260 prayers to pray specifically and intentionally for your children. These easy "mustard seed" size prayers are just the beginning to greater conversations with God and of your children's growth in godly character.

Each prayer is rooted in and echoes God's perfect Word; each Bible verse sets forth one godly characteristic God desires your children to develop. Between the Bible verse and the prayer is a brief devotion offering inspiration, instruction, or an idea to consider.

Page by page, *A Mother's Prayers* furnishes simple prayers you can repeat throughout the day or use as a springboard to deeper encounters with God. Use *A Mother's Prayers* to get you started praying for your children. Let God speak to you through each Bible verse and learn from him. Focus your prayers so you can see God's answers. Nurture your children's faith with prayer and God's Word. Teach your children God's truths. In short, *plant seeds of faith and character through prayer.* Let *A Mother's Prayers for Her Children* transform your prayers from vague and general requests to specific and distinct petitions in line with God's will for your children's lives.

Let the word of Christ dwell in you richly.

COLOSSIANS 3:16

Faithful

Be faithful until death,
and I will give you the crown of life.

REVELATION 2:10 NRSV

L ife at death! This ironic godly twist is
what Jesus promises if you are faithful
in your Christian walk. Are you growing in
faith and steadfastly moving toward your
crown of life?

Jesus, keep my children faithful
so that at their death they may receive
the crown of life. Amen.

Devoted to Prayer

Devote yourselves to prayer,
being watchful and thankful.

COLOSSIANS 4:2

How dedicated are you to prayer?
How does it compare to your
dedication to your children, spouse, or work?
Are you making time to be in conversation
with God throughout your day, being
watchful for his answers and thankful for his
many blessings?

Lord Jesus, encourage my children
to be devoted to prayer,
being watchful for your answers
and thankful for your blessings. Amen.

Careful

Be very careful, then, how you live—
not as unwise but as wise,
making the most of every opportunity,
because the days are evil.

Ephesians 5:15-16

In the blink of an eye your children will grow up and leave your house. Time is short. Be diligent to use every opportunity to tell your children about Jesus and living a holy life.

Lord, open my eyes to every opportunity
to teach my children about you,
and help my children to be careful
how they live because the days
are evil. Amen.

Holy

You must be holy, because I am holy.

1 Peter 1:16 NCV

God wants you to be set apart in humble distinction from the world's sinful ways. Actively train your children in holiness by displaying God's standard in the books you read, the movies you attend, the language you use, and the company you keep. Let your life and the choices you make testify to your commitment to holiness.

Holy God, fill my children with the desire to be holy as you are holy. Amen.

On Guard

*Therefore, dear friends, since you
already know this, be on your guard
so that you may not be carried away
by the error of lawless men
and fall from your secure position.*

2 PETER 3:17

Be on guard for the faith! Godless people
will distort Scripture and twist its truths.
Give your children a solid understanding of
biblical truths so they will not be deceived.

*Father, protect my children from
deception and being carried away by the
error of lawless people.
Keep them secure in the faith.
Amen.*

Born Again

You should not be surprised at my saying, "You must be born again."

To the unbeliever the notion of being born again is ridiculous. However, to the believer it is essential. You are born again into the kingdom of God if you have repented of your sins and put your trust in Jesus.

❋

Heavenly Father, arouse in my children a need to be born again by repenting and putting their trust in you. Amen.

Mature

*Don't be childish in your understanding
of these things. Be innocent as babies
when it comes to evil, but be mature and
wise in understanding matters of this kind.*

1 CORINTHIANS 14:20 NLT

Don't be a spiritual infant. It is time to
grow up spiritually and know God
personally. Begin by reading your Bible to
learn about God and his desires for you, and
then develop a daily prayer life seeking the
Holy Spirit's wisdom.

*Mighty God, grant my children
a mature faith and wisdom to discern
your truths. Amen.*

Joyful

Make a joyful noise to God,
all the earth; sing the glory of his name;
give to him glorious praise.

PSALM 66:1-2 NRSV

Coincidence is a nonbeliever's way of explaining God-appointed encounters. God has ordered every detail of your life. Open your eyes to see God at work and make a joyful noise in recognition of what he is doing.

O God, open my children's eyes
to see you working in their lives and fill
them with a joyful noise to you. Amen.

Generous

All goes well for those who are generous,
who lend freely and conduct their business fairly.

PSALM 112:5 NLT

You are God's manager of all he has
given to you, and he expects you to be
fair and generous. Remember that your
business is really God's business. If he were to
audit your work today, how would you fare?

Father, help my children
be generous, lend freely, and conduct
their business fairly. Amen.

Beautiful

*It is not fancy hair, gold jewelry, or fine clothes
that should make you beautiful. No, your
beauty should come from within you—
the beauty of a gentle and quiet spirit that will
never be destroyed and is very precious to God.*

1 PETER 3:3-4 NCV

Unlike the world's value of physical
appearance, God does not judge beauty
by your body shape or clothing style. God
looks to your heart for the beauty of a gentle
and quiet spirit. If you fully trust in Christ,
you are beautiful.

*God our Creator, give my children
assurance that true beauty is not the
physical beauty portrayed in magazines
or movies, but rather the inner beauty of
a gentle and quiet spirit inspired
by your love. Amen.*

Walk in Truth

I have no greater joy than to hear that my children are walking in the truth.

3 JOHN 4

We desire many things for our children—happiness, good grades, financial security, and personal safety. But no greater joy can you have than to know your children have a personal relationship with Jesus Christ. What are you doing to help your children make a decision for Christ and to live life for him?

*Gracious God, lead my children
to know you as their Lord and Savior
and to walk in your truth.
Amen.*

Thankful

*It is good to give thanks to the Lord, to
sing praises to your name, O Most High;
to declare your steadfast love in the
morning, and your faithfulness by night.*

PSALM 92:1-2 NRSV

Much of life is taken for granted. Look
around and give thanks for all things
small and big. Thank God for erasers,
refrigerator magnets, your child's touch, and
the saving knowledge of Jesus Christ.

*Lord, create a thankful heart in my
children for every detail in their
lives and a longing to sing praises to you
from morning until night.
Amen.*

Love Neighbor

*Don't seek vengeance. Don't bear
a grudge; but love your
neighbor as yourself, for I am Jehovah.*

LEVITICUS 19:18 TLB

D o you have an irritating neighbor?
Do your children see you lending a
hand in love to that neighbor or picking
fights and planning your next barrage of
insults? Let your child see you love even
those who are hard to love.

*Jehovah God, let your
example of love teach my
children to love their
neighbor. Amen.*

Saved

Turn to me and be saved,
all you ends of the earth; for I am God,
and there is no other.

ISAIAH 45:22

Turn. That is all you need to do to
be saved. Turn from your sins—
your disobedience and your self-reliance—
and turn to God, for there is no other.

Lord God, turn my children
to you to be saved. Give them the
assurance that you are the only true God
and there is no other. Amen.

Watchful

*Keep a close watch on all you do and
think. Stay true to what is right and God
will bless you and use you to help others.*

1 TIMOTHY 4:16 TLB

When children are nearby, we take
more notice of inappropriate words
and actions in TV shows, movies, and songs.
At other times, we become numb to the
persistent presence of foul language and
impure behavior. As God's child, stay true to
what is right, be watchful of spiritual danger,
and stand firm in the faith.

*Savior, keep my children watchful
for spiritual danger, courageous to do
what is right, and useful
to you to help others. Amen.*

Happy

Happy are those who trust in the Lord.

PROVERBS 16:20 NRSV

Temporary happiness may come in a Happy Meal, video game, or Disney vacation. However, eternal happiness certainly comes to those who trust in the Lord. Be sure your children know the difference.

*Loving God, remind my children
that happiness comes to
those who trust in you. Amen.*

Wise

If any of you lacks wisdom, he should ask God, who gives generously to all without finding fault, and it will be given to him.

Do you worry if you are raising your children right? Your first step to parental wisdom should be toward your Heavenly Father. Meet God in prayer and Scripture, and he will generously give you wisdom without finding fault.

Lord, I pray for wisdom to raise my children and wisdom for my children to discern your ways. Amen.

Alert

*Be self-controlled and alert. Your enemy
the devil prowls around like a
roaring lion looking for someone to devour.*

1 PETER 5:8

Make no mistake about it, the devil is
real and desires your soul. Keep alert
and recognize the lures and trappings of evil.
Flee worldly sins drawing you away from
God by reaching out to God for help to
exercise self-control.

*Mighty Lord, safeguard my children
from the evils of this world that
prowl around like a roaring lion looking
for someone to devour. Amen.*

Blameless

*Do everything without complaining or
arguing, so that you may become blameless
and pure, children of God.*

PHILIPPIANS 2:14-15

Do you find yourself refereeing your
children's arguments? Teach your
children to calmly and respectfully resolve
conflict with an understanding that God
wants them to live in Christian unity.
Help your children be blameless by extending
the hand of fellowship in Christ.

*Holy God, encourage my children to do
everything without complaining or
arguing, so they may become blameless
and pure children of God. Amen.*

Restored

Restore me, and I will return,
because you are the Lord my God.

JEREMIAH 31:18

Spiritual restoration begins with confession and repentance of all sin. Through Christ's death on the cross, forgiveness is freely given. Christ paid the penalty for your sins so that a holy, righteous relationship with him is restored.

Jesus, bring to my children's minds
their sins so they may seek your
forgiveness and be restored. Amen.

Worshipful

Come, let us bow down in worship,
let us kneel before the Lord our Maker.

PSALM 95:6

Worship is not limited to Sundays. Come and worship the Lord each day, glorifying him in thought, word, and deed. Let your daily worship spill over into your children's lives so they too may experience a lifetime of worship.

Lord of my life, inspire my children
to bow down and
worship you each day. Amen.

Welcoming

*And whoever welcomes a little
child like this in my name welcomes me.*

MATTHEW 18:5

Do you gladly welcome your children
or do you turn them away because
you are tired or too busy? Sit down with
your children today and welcome their
stories, ideas, and love. Know that the
example you set with your children will be
passed on to your grandchildren.

*Jesus, do not let my actions
turn away my children. Through me,
teach my children to welcome everyone
in your name. Amen.*

Avoid Arguments

*Again I say, don't get involved
in foolish arguments which only upset
people and make them angry.*

2 TIMOTHY 2:23 TLB

Your relationship with your child is more important than winning a minor point. Avoid arguments over the trivial. Foolish arguments, no matter who starts them, produce few winners.

*O Lord, keep my children and me
from foolish arguments that only upset
us and make us angry. Amen.*

Please God

*We are not trying to please
men but God, who tests our hearts.*

1 Thessalonians 2:4

Children are tempted to compromise their Christian values in an effort to fit in with their peers. Yet it is God to whom they are accountable. Create in your children a desire to please God before pleasing their friends.

*Holy God, shield my children
from trying to please
others more than you. Amen.*

Worthy

*Only, live your life in a manner
worthy of the gospel of Christ.*

PHILIPPIANS 1:27 NRSV

Jesus Christ died for your sins. Are you
living your life in a manner worthy of
Christ's sacrifice? Are you teaching your
children to reflect his exceptional character?

*Lord Jesus, motivate my children
to live their life in a manner worthy
of the gospel. Amen.*

Sexually Pure

But among you there must not be even
a hint of sexual immorality, or of any kind
of impurity, or of greed, because these are
improper for God's holy people.

EPHESIANS 5:3

Where do you draw the line to maintain sexual purity? It is before there is even a hint of sexual immorality. Draw that line for your children.

Holy God, protect my children
from sexual temptation.
Let there not be even a hint of
sexual immorality. Amen.

Remember Sabbath

*Remember the Sabbath day
by keeping it holy.*

Exodus 20:8

Are you rearranging your weekly worship to accommodate a child's sports activity? What message are you sending to your children when a hockey or basketball game is more important than worshiping together? Maybe it is time to take a stand for God and rearrange your priorities.

Righteous Lord, help my children to remember to put you first and to keep a weekly holy day to worship you. Amen.

Strong

*Be strong in the faith, just as
you were taught, and always be thankful.*

COLOSSIANS 2:7 NCV

Spiritual strength comes by exercising
your faith daily. Build up your faith
muscles by studying the Bible, meeting God
in prayer, and trusting God to meet your
needs. Equip your children to encounter
God each day and teach them to always
be thankful.

*Mighty God, keep my children strong
in the faith, just as they were taught,
and to always be thankful. Amen.*

Fulfilled

The Lord will fulfill his purpose for me.
PSALM 138:8

Worthy as your future goals may be, God's goals are the only perfect purpose for you. Let God's purposes flow through you. Seek God's guidance, be attentive for his answer, and be available to his call.

Lord, give my children insight into your purpose for them and help them to be obedient to your calling. Amen.

Righteous

The righteous will live by faith.
ROMANS 1:17

Once you commit your life to Christ, how you live it is simple. You live it for God. Start now by stepping out in faith— maybe even out of your comfort zone—and tell a friend about Jesus.

Redeemer Lord, you have made us righteous. Help my children to step out in faith to advance your kingdom. Amen.

Imitator

Be imitators of God.

EPHESIANS 5:1

We imitate those we love. What does your behavior reveal about your love for God? Do your children see God reflected in you each day?

Holy God, invigorate my children to be imitators of you. Amen.

Gracious

Let your speech always be gracious,
seasoned with salt, so that you may know
how you ought to answer everyone.

COLOSSIANS 4:6 NRSV

Word choice, tone, and attitude affect
communication. How you present
the message of Jesus Christ will either
encourage people to listen or turn them away.
Seek God's guidance to graciously share
your faith.

Help my children, O Lord,
to speak graciously as well as sensibly,
so that they may know
how to answer everyone. Amen.

Pursue Peace

*Let us then pursue what makes for peace
and for mutual upbuilding.*

ROMANS 14:19 NRSV

World peace begins at home.
Teach your children to pursue peace
and build each other up in love by speaking
graciously and acting kindly. Children who
experience harmony at home learn to extend
it into the rest of the world.

*Almighty God, encourage my children
to pursue those activities
that make for peace and for mutual
upbuilding and let their pursuit of peace
begin at home. Amen.*

Content

*Keep your lives free from the love of
money and be content with what you
have, because God has said, "Never will I
leave you; never will I forsake you."*

Hebrews 13:5

How much more do you need to be
happy? Dissatisfaction can breed
whether you desire a little or a lot. Be
content knowing that God provides for your
needs and is always with you.

*Heavenly Father, whether our family
has much or little, help my children
to be content with what we
have, knowing that you
are with us always.
Amen.*

Wait Expectantly

I wait for the Lord, my soul waits,
and in his word I put my hope.

PSALM 130:5

Each spring, tulips and daffodils that were planted the previous autumn push up through the cold ground to display their beauty. Like spring flowers, God's answers to prayers may not come in the season in which they were prayed. Waiting for answers is difficult if we forget that God's timing is always perfect.

Sovereign Lord, encourage my children
to wait expectantly for the answers
to their prayers and to put
their hope in you, knowing your timing
is perfect. Amen.

Openhanded to Poor

Do not be hardhearted or tightfisted
toward your poor brother.
Rather be openhanded and
freely lend him whatever he needs.

<small>DEUTERONOMY 15:7-8</small>

Everything we have is from God. If you
are blessed with time, volunteer; if given
special talents, use them to glorify God;
if provided with wealth, share with the less
fortunate. Be openhanded to all God's children.

Father, protect my children from
being hardhearted or tightfisted toward
the poor; lead them
to be openhanded and freely lend
to those in need. Amen.

Diligent

*You have commanded
your precepts to be kept diligently.*

PSALM 119:4 NRSV

Dentists remind us to diligently brush
our teeth to prevent tooth decay.
Similarly, to prevent spiritual decay we must
come clean before the Lord, diligently
confessing our disobedience and meeting
him daily in prayer and Scripture. A good
parent teaches her children to brush daily; a
godly parent teaches her children to confess,
pray, and read the Bible daily.

*Excite my children to diligently
obey you, O Lord, and stir up a passion
to meet you in your Word and
in prayer each day. Amen.*

Forgiving

If someone does wrong to you, forgive that person because the Lord forgave you.

Colossians 3:13 NCV

I t is hard to forgive. But remember, God forgave you by sending his Son to pay the death sentence for your sins. Ask God to give you the strength through Christ to forgive as he has forgiven you.

*Merciful Savior,
remind my children to forgive as you
have forgiven them. Amen.*

Know Christ

For I resolved to know nothing
while I was with you except Jesus Christ
and him crucified.

1 CORINTHIANS 2:2

More than intellectual knowledge is needed to really know Jesus. Even the devil knows about Jesus. To have a saving knowledge of Jesus, you must surrender your life to him alone and live in obedience for him.

Lord, give to my children
a saving knowledge of Jesus Christ
and him crucified. Amen.

Honor God
With Wealth

*Honor the Lord with your wealth,
with the first fruits of all your crops; then
your barns will be filled to overflowing, and
your vats will brim over with new wine.*

PROVERBS 3:9-10

Do not give your leftovers to God.
Trust God to provide for all your
needs by obediently giving to him first from
your paycheck. Honor God with your wealth
and he will bless you with abundance.

*God of abundance, teach my children
to honor you with their first fruits
and assure them that they will
receive blessings in return. Amen.*

Equipped to Do God's Will

And now may the God of peace,
who brought again from the dead our
Lord Jesus, equip you with
all you need for doing his will.

HEBREWS 13:20-21 TLB

God does not call the equipped; he equips
the called. Ask God what he wants
you to do. Then be amazed at how he
provides you with all you need for doing it.

Mighty God, lead my children to seek
your guidance for their life and to know
that you have equipped them with all
they need for doing your will. Amen.

Faithful Servant

Well done, good and faithful servant!

MATTHEW 25:21

Children love to hear their parents' praise for doing a good job. As an obedient child of God we too look forward to hearing God's commendation. Imagine the day our Holy God welcomes us to heaven saying, "Well done, good and faithful servant!"

Heavenly Father, stir up a desire in my children to faithfully serve you so when they are welcomed into your kingdom you will say, "Well done, good and faithful servant!" Amen.

Patient

Be patient with everyone.

1 THESSALONIANS 5:14

G od has shown great patience with you. You sin against him time and time again, and yet he keeps forgiving and loving you. Seek his patience when your children try your own.

Almighty God, teach my children to be patient with everyone. Amen.

Show No Favoritism

As believers in our glorious
Lord Jesus Christ, don't show favoritism.

JAMES 2:1

The fastest way to crush a child's spirit
is to favor one child over another.
Jesus loves us all equally; he has no favorites.
Love each of your children as Jesus loves you.

Dear Jesus, as believers keep
my children from showing favoritism
and give to them the ability to lovingly
treat all people equally. Amen.

Strive for God

For to this end we toil and strive,
because we have our hope set
on the living God, who is the Savior
of all men, especially of those who believe.

1 TIMOTHY 4:10 RSV

Raising godly children doesn't happen without effort. Children left to find God on their own usually don't. Therefore, toil and strive to lead your children into a personal relationship with Jesus Christ.

Living God, urge my children to strive
to bring others to the knowledge of
eternal life through faith in you. Amen.

Clear Minded

The end of all things is near.
Therefore be clear minded and
self-controlled so that you can pray.

1 PETER 4:7

Our youth are inundated with violent
and sexual images from TV shows,
video games, magazines, and movies.
Their minds capture the image and replay it
without warning. Keep your children's minds
clear from ungodly images by establishing
rules for what they can see and teaching
them to honor God in their choices.

Holy God, keep my children clear
minded and help them to use self-control
so they can pray and make godly choices.
Amen.

Hold Unswervingly to Faith

*Let us hold unswervingly to the hope
we profess, for he who promised is faithful.*

HEBREWS 10:23

Children can be easily swayed in their
beliefs. Give your children a firm
foundation of biblical truths so they know
with confidence what they believe and why.
Help them hold unswervingly to Jesus Christ.

*Jesus, strengthen my children
to hold unswervingly to the hope they
profess, for you are faithful
to your promises. Amen.*

Fruit of the Spirit

*By contrast, the fruit of the Spirit is love,
joy, peace, patience, kindness, generosity,
faithfulness, gentleness, and self-control.*

GALATIANS 5:22-23 NRSV

A Spirit-filled believer demonstrates love,
joy, peace, patience, kindness,
generosity, faithfulness, gentleness, and self-
control. By contrast, someone without the
Holy Spirit displays hate, dread, agitation,
anxiousness, thoughtlessness, stinginess,
disloyalty, gruffness, and unrestraint. Let the
Holy Spirit dwell richly in you so that God's
presence is evident to all.

*O God, fill my children with
the fruit of the Spirit. Prompt them to
show love, joy, peace, patience, kindness,
generosity, faithfulness, gentleness,
and self-control. Amen.*

Sincere Heart

*Let us draw near to God with a
sincere heart in full assurance of faith.*

HEBREWS 10:22

Salvation is a gift from God. In response,
meet God today and each day through
prayer and his Word. Come to him with a
true heart of love and know with certainty
that you have eternal life.

*Help my children to draw near to you,
Eternal God, with a sincere heart in full
assurance of faith. Amen.*

No Evil Talk

Let no evil talk come out of your mouths,
but only what is useful for building up,
as there is need, so that your
words may give grace to those who hear.

Ephesians 4:29 nrsv

Each word spoken in love or anger strikes deep within your children's hearts and souls. If what you intend to express is not useful for building up your loved one, then do not say it. Let your words be a reflection of God's love and give grace to those who hear them.

Lord Jesus, let no evil talk come out
of my children's mouths. May their words
give grace to all who hear. Amen.

Confess Sins

*I said, "I will confess my sins
to the Lord," and you forgave my guilt.*

PSALM 32:5 NCV

Admitting you are wrong is difficult.
But broken relationships with others
and with God are only restored after
confessing your sinfulness. Come to God
with a broken heart for your disobedience,
and he will forgive all your sins and cleanse
you from all unrighteousness.

*When my children do wrong, Lord,
pester them to confess their sins and
receive your forgiveness. Amen.*

Do Right

*So let us not grow weary in doing
what is right, for we will reap
at harvest-time, if we do not give up.*

GALATIANS 6:9 NRSV

Sometimes making the right and godly choice is not easy because such a choice is not valued by the world. When weariness in doing what is right prevails, keep focused on the fact that God has saved you from an eternity in hell. Let God's grace motivate you to keep doing what is right.

*Lord Jesus, strengthen my children
so they will not grow weary
in doing what is right. Amen.*

Boastful in the Lord

Let the one who boasts, boast in the Lord.
2 CORINTHIANS 10:17 NRSV

In our efforts to develop our children's self-esteem, we puff them up with unyielding praise. Do we also infuse a spirit of crediting God for their success? Teach your children that God blesses them with talent so that all boasting must be in the Lord.

*Gracious God, give to my children
the understanding that all things come
from you so that all boasting
is in you. Amen.*

Peacemaker

Blessed are the peacemakers,
for they will be called children of God.

MATTHEW 5:9 NRSV

Victims of bullying, harassment, and
violence need others to come alongside
to support and stand up for them. Now is
the time to prepare our children to be
peacemakers. This generation can make a
difference and receive the blessing of being
peacemakers and children of God.

Father, in this conflicted world
may my children be peacemakers among
their peers and all people. Amen.

Zealous

*Never be lacking in zeal, but keep
your spiritual fervor, serving the Lord.*

ROMANS 12:11

If you do something enough times it
becomes routine. You may pass the offering
plate without considering your gratitude to
God or recite the Lord's Prayer without
thinking about what you have said. To keep
your spiritual fervor and zealously serve God,
remember the Cross, stay in God's Word,
pray unceasingly, and worship reverently.

*Most Holy God, keep my children
zealous to know you as their Savior and
to serve you each day. Amen.*

Hospitable

*Offer hospitality to
one another without grumbling.*

1 PETER 4:9

Do you fail to offer hospitality because
it is not convenient or requires an
effort to get ready? God wants us to
graciously welcome others into our lives and
homes so that we may be witnesses to God's
love and mercy. Show your children the
virtue of hospitality by scheduling today that
dinner invitation you have been putting off.

*Jesus, through my example, teach my
children to offer hospitality to
one another without grumbling. Amen.*

Matched
With Believers

Do not be mismatched with unbelievers.
For what partnership is there between
righteousness and lawlessness?... Or what
does a believer share with an unbeliever?

2 CORINTHIANS 6:14-15 NRSV

The friendship and marriage bond is
strongest when a love for God Almighty
is shared. What a blessing it is when spiritual
matters are freely discussed and God's will is
sought through unified prayer. Teach your
children the blessings received when God is
the focal point of any relationship, but
especially in marriage.

O Lord, help my children to understand
the importance of being matched
with a believer. Bring a godly mate into
my children's lives. Amen.

Overcome Unbelief

I do believe;
help me overcome my unbelief.

MARK 9:24

Sometimes unbelief may steal into your
heart. In these moments of doubt,
don't deny it—confess it. God is faithful
and will come to your aid to help you
overcome unbelief.

Merciful God, when doubts
assail my children, urge them to call out
to you for help saying, "I believe,
help me overcome my unbelief." Amen.

Witness

But you will receive power when the
Holy Spirit comes on you; and you will be
my witnesses...to the ends of the earth.

ACTS 1:8

Jesus' disciples were eyewitnesses to his life, death, resurrection, and ascension. It is through these eyewitnesses that God's message of salvation comes to you. Now it is your turn to go and be a witness of Jesus living in you.

Father, empower my children with
your Holy Spirit to be a bold
witness for you all the days
of their lives. Amen.

Conqueror

If you conquer, you will be clothed
like them in white robes, and I will not
blot your name out of the book of life;
I will confess your name
before my Father and before his angels.

REVELATION 3:5 NRSV

Through spiritual battles, Satan fights to keep your name out of God's book of life. However, Jesus has already won the war. With Jesus on your side, you will be a conqueror and Jesus will be confessing your name as part of his victorious spiritual army.

Mighty God, uphold my children
to be conquerors of the faith
and to someday hear their names
confessed before you. Amen.

Stand Firm

But he who stands
firm to the end will be saved.

MATTHEW 24:13

While society's values are in constant flux, God's truths are unchanging. Stand firm in God's Word to avoid worldly confusion of what is right and wrong. God promises that if you stand firm to the end— end of time or end of your life—you will be saved.

Lord, strengthen my children
to stand firm in their faith until the
end of time. Amen.

Ambassador

So we are ambassadors for Christ,
since God is making his appeal through
us; we entreat you on behalf
of Christ, be reconciled to God.

2 CORINTHIANS 5:20 NRSV

You are Christ's ambassador. God has appointed you to represent his kingdom to all people. As God's ambassador, go and tell the Gospel message, beginning with your children.

Almighty God, create an excitement in
my children that they are your
ambassadors. Encourage them
to bring your message of
salvation to the people
you put in their path
each day. Amen.

Hot Faith

*I know what you do, that you are not
hot or cold. I wish that you were hot or cold!*

REVELATION 3:15 NCV

A faith neither on fire for the Lord nor
stone cold has just enough religious
piety to make lukewarm believers think their
nominal relationship with God is just fine.
However, a lukewarm faith is no faith at all.
Do not be deceived.

*Lord, stoke my children's faith so it is
red hot for you. Amen.*

Nonjudgmental

You, therefore, have no excuse, you who pass judgment on someone else, for at whatever point you judge the other, you are condemning yourself, because you who pass judgment do the same things.

ROMANS 2:1

I t is easy to judge the behaviors and actions of others. However, it is so difficult to see our own failures! Everyone has fallen short of what God expects, so take a good look in the mirror before passing judgment, and remember to love others as God loves you.

Heavenly Father, direct my children not to judge others but instead to love as you have loved us. Amen.

Courageous

Be strong, and let your heart take courage,
all you who wait for the Lord.

PSALM 31:24 NRSV

Sometimes our faith falters when earnest prayers are not answered immediately or as we would like. At these times, we need to keep reading the Bible, hang on to the promises of God, and pray unceasingly. In other words, be strong, take courage, and wait for the Lord.

Lord, fortify my children's faith
so they are strong and their hearts
take courage as they stand firm
in their hope in you. Amen.

Respectful

Show respect for everyone.
1 PETER 2:17 NLT

Traditional manners are slowly eroding.
The trend is to be more casual.
Nevertheless, teach your children that
showing respect for everyone is always in
style with God.

*Jesus, persuade my children
to show respect to everyone. Amen.*

Keep a Strong Grip

With all these things in mind, dear brothers and sisters, stand firm and keep a strong grip on everything we taught you both in person and by letter.

2 THESSALONIANS 2:15 NLT

When your children go off to school or college they will encounter new ideas. Teachers, friends, and ideas may challenge what you have taught them. Warn your children to keep a strong grip on their faith and continue to support their spiritual growth.

Almighty God, encourage my children to stand firm and to keep a strong grip on everything I have taught them about your truths. Amen.

Obey Government

Obey the government, for God is
the one who has put it there.
There is no government anywhere that
God has not placed in power.

ROMANS 13:1 TLB

G od has established every government.
You must respect the office even if
you do not respect the officer. Life without
laws becomes chaos.

God, thank you for our government.
Guide my children to become good
citizens who act responsibly within the
governing laws. Amen.

Integrity

I know, my God, that you test the heart
and are pleased with integrity.

1 Chronicles 29:17

It is difficult to teach integrity when stock
scandals, corporate corruption, and
government abuses appear to be common
practice. Even though this world may not
always value integrity, God does. For this
reason alone, strive for integrity each day.

Holy God, cultivate integrity
within my children so that
when you test their
hearts you will be
pleased. Amen.

Not Anxious

Do not be anxious about anything,
but in everything, by prayer and petition,
with thanksgiving,
present your requests to God.

PHILIPPIANS 4:6

Worry shows lack of faith in Almighty God and pulls you away from him. Draw near to God in prayer and lay your burdens before him to conquer your anxieties. With a thankful heart you can know that God is in control of all things.

Mighty Lord, when my children
are anxious, remind them to bring their
concerns to you and to rejoice in
your sovereign control over all things.
Amen.

Choose to Serve God

You must choose for yourselves today whom you will serve.... As for me and my family, we will serve the Lord.

JOSHUA 24:15 NCV

The fact that you are a Christian does not automatically make your children Christians as well. Lead your children to Jesus so they can choose for themselves to serve him as their personal Lord and Savior. Help them understand that by grace God offers salvation to all who repent and believe.

Almighty God, I know that you have chosen my children. In response, prompt my children to choose for themselves today to serve Jesus forever. Amen.

Competent

*Not that we are competent in ourselves
to claim anything for ourselves,
but our competence comes from God.*

2 CORINTHIANS 3:5

Lack of confidence prevents people from boldly moving forward in work or play. If we focus on our own abilities, we are rightly incompetent. However, when we focus on God's power leading us, we may proceed with godly competence in his service.

*All-Knowing God, grant
to my children godly
competence to use their
talents in ministry
for you. Amen.*

Spotless

*Make every effort to be found spotless,
blameless and at peace with [God].*

2 PETER 3:14

Daily effort is required to keep a house
spotless. It is also an effort to keep your
life free from worldly filth. Come to Jesus
each day for strength to keep out the squalor
and to receive cleansing from your sins.

*Motivate my children, Lord,
to come to you to clean up their lives so
they may be found spotless, blameless,
and at peace with you. Amen.*

Pray in the Spirit

But you, dear friends,
build yourselves up in your most holy
faith and pray in the Holy Spirit.
JUDE 20

Praying in the Holy Spirit allows you to be in the presence of God even when you don't know what to say. The Holy Spirit controls your life and knows your every need. Praise God that he is always with you.

Holy Spirit, come into
my children's lives and fill them with
your presence. Amen.

No Bad Company

Do not be misled:
"Bad company corrupts good character."

1 CORINTHIANS 15:33

Who your children choose as friends is important. Your child's reputation can be destroyed through actual corruption or the mere association with the corrupt. Neither is acceptable, so warn your children to stay clear of bad company.

Lord, guide my children to choose their friends wisely and protect them from bad company. Amen.

Qualified

*Giving thanks to the Father, who has
qualified you to share in the inheritance
of the saints in the kingdom of light.*

COLOSSIANS 1:12

There are no tryouts. You qualify to
spend eternity with Jesus. Not because
of your own efforts, but because Jesus paid
the penalty for your sins by dying on the
cross for you.

*Thank you, Lord Jesus,
for qualifying my children to spend
eternity with you. Amen.*

Rich in Good Deeds

Command them to do good,
to be rich in good deeds, and to be
generous and willing to share.

1 TIMOTHY 6:18

D on't shut your eyes to the needy.
Let God speak to your heart and then
take action. Be rich in good deeds by making
the most of every opportunity to serve others.

O Lord, open my children's eyes
to those in need and help them to be
rich in good deeds. Amen.

Reconciled

But now he has reconciled you by Christ's
physical body through death
to present you holy in his sight, without
blemish and free from accusation.

Y ou had a complete relationship break-
up with God. You were sinful,
unacceptable to God. However, Jesus' death
made you perfect in God's sight and your
relationship has been reconciled forever.

Heavenly Father, thank you for
reconciling my children's relationship
with you through Jesus. Amen.

Honor Marriage

*Marriage should be honored by all,
and the marriage bed kept pure, for God
will judge the adulterer and all the
sexually immoral.*

Hebrews 13:4

The marriage vow is sacred and to be honored for a lifetime. Infidelity and sexual immorality dishonors God and your mate. Stress to your children the value God places on marriage and the purity required before marriage and after.

*Holy God, keep my children sexually
pure before and after marriage. Amen.*

Harvest Worker

The harvest is plentiful,
but the workers are few. Ask the Lord of
the harvest, therefore, to send
out workers into his harvest field.

LUKE 10:2

The field of unbelievers is plentiful, but those willing to invite them into God's family are few. Be a harvest worker. Tell your faith story to unbelievers, invite them to church or ask them to join your Bible study.

Eternal God, I give my children
to you to be harvest workers. Send them
wherever you see a need. Amen.

Unified

May they be brought to complete
unity to let the world know
that you sent me and have loved them
even as you have loved me.

JOHN 17:23

Jesus prayed for your complete unity with
believers. Why? So the unbelieving world
would see God's love for all people through
the love shown by you and fellow believers.

Father, unify my children so their
love for each other will testify to the love
you have for all people. Amen.

Wonderfully Made

*I praise you because I am fearfully
and wonderfully made; your works are
wonderful, I know that full well.*

PSALM 139:14

The complexity of the human body
shouts of a Master Creator. Introduce
your children to God by showing them how
wonderfully they are made. Praise God
together for his hand in every detail of life.

*Almighty God, Creator of all,
inspire my children to praise you for
your creation and for how fearfully and
wonderfully you made them. Amen.*

Follow the Way

*Jesus answered, "I am the
way and the truth and the life."*

JOHN 14:6

Lost in life? Don't know where you are
heading? Take directions from Jesus
who says, "I am the way and the truth and
the life."

*Jesus, we are lost without you.
You are the answer to life's
questions and problems.
Lead my children in your direction and
teach them your truths. Amen.*

Completed Good Work

I am confident of this, that the one who began a good work among you will bring it to completion by the day of Jesus Christ.

PHILIPPIANS 1:6 NRSV

God always finishes what he starts. In fact, the job of salvation has been accomplished and God's plan for your life will be completed at Jesus' second coming. You can be confident that God will not leave you—his workmanship—half finished.

Lord, give my children the confidence to know that you who began a good work in them will bring it to completion when you come again. Amen.

Love

Love is patient; love is kind; love is not
envious or boastful or arrogant or rude.
It does not insist on its own way; it is not
irritable or resentful; it does not rejoice in
wrongdoing, but rejoices in the truth.
It bears all things, believes all things, hopes
all things, endures all things.

1 CORINTHIANS 13:4-7 NRSV

Wouldn't it be wonderful to have
these verses come to mind every time
your children push you to the limits of your
patience? Burn God's Word into your memory
and inscribe it on your heart so in a moment's
notice you will recall it.

Lord God, help my children to learn
the true meaning of love and
may they learn it through me. Amen.

Glad

*I was glad when they said to me,
"Let us go to the house of the Lord!"*
PSALM 122:1 NRSV

Do you enthusiastically build up going to church the way you do a trip to Grandma's house? This week, talk to your children about how glad you are to meet with fellow believers and to spend time worshiping, praising, and thanking God. Stir up excitement to worship your Mighty God!

*Lord, create in my children
an eager anticipation to go to church
and to worship you. Amen.*

Provided
in Abundance

And God is able to provide you with every
blessing in abundance, so that by always
having enough of everything, you may share
abundantly in every good work.

2 CORINTHIANS 9:8 NRSV

Giving to God won't deplete you. In fact, using God's math, subtraction becomes addition and even multiplication. The more you give the more God provides so that you may share generously with others.

God of all goodness, assure my children
that you provide for all their needs
and more so they may
joyfully share with others. Amen.

No Room
for the Devil

And do not make room for the devil.

EPHESIANS 4:27 NRSV

Holding a grudge opens the door for the devil to enter your life and cause you to sin. Shut out the devil by quickly resolving your differences with others, and especially with your children. Confess your wrongs or extend forgiveness before the devil gets a foothold.

Mighty Lord, keep my children safe from giving the devil any opportunity to take up residency. Amen.

Merciful

Be merciful, just as
your Father is merciful.

LUKE 6:36

To be as merciful as God is a high calling. God's mercy for us was so great that he did not spare his own Son the agony of death on a cross. If you have accepted God's mercy, how can you not extend similar mercy?

Father, fill my children with
your mercy that they, in turn, will
extend mercy to others. Amen.

Fear God

Happy are those who fear the Lord,
who greatly delight in his commandments.

PSALM 112:1 NRSV

If you personally know God, you have a
reverent fear of him and delight to do his
will. If you don't know him as Lord and
Savior, come to him now and give him your
life. What happiness there is for those who
belong to God.

Lord, teach my children to fear you
with reverent awe and
to delight in your Word. Amen.

Do All Things Through Christ

I can do all things through Christ,
because he gives me strength.

PHILIPPIANS 4:13 NCV

God has a plan for your life and he intends to see it through to completion. If Almighty God is leading the way, you cannot fail. In moments of panic, go to God in prayer, do all that you can do, and depend on God to do the rest.

Dear Jesus, fortify my children with the
understanding that they can do all
things in your will through
your strength and power.
Amen.

Persevere

Let us run with perseverance
the race marked out for us.
Let us fix our eyes on Jesus, the author
and perfecter of our faith.

HEBREWS 12:1-2

A marathon is only completed after much preparation, training, and perseverance. In your Christian race, you must persevere through life's struggles and prepare yourself to meet Christ. Spiritual perseverance requires setting your sights on Jesus and training yourself in God's character through Bible study and prayer.

Jesus, as my children's faith coach,
help me to train them to run life's race
with perseverance toward you so that
they fix their eyes on you, stay in your
Word, and come to you in prayer. Amen.

Redeemed

*In him we have redemption through his
blood, the forgiveness of sins, in
accordance with the riches of God's grace.*

EPHESIANS 1:7

Jesus has brought you back into his
kingdom. Through Christ's death and
resurrection, you have forgiveness of sins and
eternal life. Right now thank God for his
grace and live for Jesus.

*Lord Jesus, thank you
for the redemption we have
through your death and resurrection.
Help my children to live as
redeemed children of God. Amen.*

Believe

*Believe on the Lord Jesus, and you
will be saved, you and your household.*

<small>ACTS 16:31 NRSV</small>

A belief in God is more than intellectual
acceptance of him. It is an active
willingness to put God first and a hunger to
know him through worship, prayer, Bible
study, and obedience. Your faithfulness will
lead your household to a saving knowledge
of Jesus Christ.

*Lead my children to believe in you,
Lord, and to put
their faith into action. Amen.*

Obedient

This is love for God;
to obey his commands.

1 JOHN 5:3

God is not a tyrant who makes you guess at the rules of life. His Word in the Bible provides all you need to know. Let the Holy Spirit teach you God's will and how it applies to your life so that you may be obedient.

God, prompt my children to
show their love for you by obeying your
commandments. Amen.

Honor Parents

Honor your father and your mother,
so that your days may be long in the land
that the Lord your God is giving you.

EXODUS 20:12 NRSV

A parent's sin against you may be stopping you from honoring your parents. Ask God to give you a heart of forgiveness. Then seek God's wisdom in raising your children so they may honor you without reserve.

Faithful Lord, help me to treat
my children justly so that they will
desire to honor me as a means
to honor you. Amen.

Move in God

*For "In him we
live and move and have our being."*

ACTS 17:28 NRSV

Y ou cannot exist apart from God.
Every breath you take, every second you
live, every move you make is because God
allows it and ordained it. Are you in tune
with God's abiding presence within you?

*Lord, make my children so much
a part of you that they may proclaim,
"In him we live and move
and have our being." Amen.*

Christian

Yet if any of you suffers as a Christian,
do not consider it a disgrace,
but glorify God because you bear this name.

<small>1 Peter 4:16 nrsv</small>

When you have troubles you can take comfort in knowing that the devil thinks of you as a worthy opponent. The devil would have no interest in you if you were part of his kingdom. Next time troubles come because you are a Christian, glorify God that the devil finds you a foe and not a friend.

Lord Jesus, let my children rejoice
that they are Christians and belong to
your Kingdom. Amen.

Not Greedy

Beware! Don't be greedy for what
you don't have. Real life is not measured
by how much we own.

LUKE 12:15 NLT

Real life—life in God—is not valued by
how many earthly possessions you have
collected. Your goal is not to gather, but to
scatter. Scatter God's Good News about Jesus.

Creator God, guard my children from
wishing for what they don't have,
and teach them that real life is not
valued by their earthly possessions. Amen.

Hopeful

But blessed are those who trust
in the Lord and have made
the Lord their hope and confidence.

JEREMIAH 17:7 NLT

Our Christian hope is not dependent on how often we attend worship, give to charities, or head up a church committee. Our hope rests solely on Jesus' blood and righteousness. If you do not have that hope within you, ask Jesus to fill your life and receive the assurance that comes when you surrender your life to him.

Almighty God, I pray that
you will be my children's
hope and confidence. Amen.

One With God

*I pray also for those who will believe in me
through [the disciples'] message,
that all of them may be one, Father, just as
you are in me and I am in you.
May they also be in us so that the world
may believe that you have sent me.*

JOHN 17:20-21

How wonderful that Jesus prayed for us as future believers! Tell your children that not only do you pray for them, but Jesus has too. Jesus prayed for our oneness with God so all the world would believe in him.

*Jesus, thank you for praying for us.
Inspire my children to exhibit
the oneness they have in you so that the
world may believe. Amen.*

Speak Truth in Love

Instead, speaking the truth in love,
we will in all things grow up into
him who is the Head, that is, Christ.

EPHESIANS 4:15

If you have a friend who does not know Christ, then it is time to speak the truth in love. The truth is, your friend is heading toward hell. In love, tell the unbeliever about Jesus dying for the sins of the world so that whoever believes in him will not perish but have everlasting life.

Savior, encourage my children to speak
the truth in love to unbelievers
about your saving grace and lead them
to your kingdom. Amen.

Righteousness
of God

*For our sake he made him to be sin who
knew no sin, so that in him we
might become the righteousness of God.*

2 CORINTHIANS 5:21 NRSV

Jesus Christ was perfect. Even though you are guilty of treason before God, Jesus paid the penalty and saved you from the death sentence. Talk to your children today about God's great love and the righteousness received through Jesus.

*Redeemer God, impart an
understanding of your righteousness to
my children. Help them grasp that
you poured their sins into your sinless
Son, Jesus, and in exchange poured your
righteousness into them. Amen.*

Press On

I press on toward the goal for the prize
of the heavenly call of God in Christ Jesus.

PHILIPPIANS 3:14 NRSV

Do you talk about God with your
children and discuss faith matters?
Have you equipped them to make God part of
their everyday life? Are you training them to
press on and trust God in good times and bad?

Jesus, help my children to press on
to that heavenly goal to be with you and to
follow your call. Amen.

Gentle

Let your gentleness be evident to all.

PHILIPPIANS 4:5

When we encounter rudeness or hostile behavior, our natural reaction is to lash out or retaliate. However, gentleness is a fruit of the Spirit and must be made evident to all. Next time someone cuts you off in traffic or skips ahead of you in line, gently give way and show your children a godly reaction.

O Lord, let my children's gentleness be evident to all and thereby bring glory to you. Amen.

Kind to Needy

*He who despises his neighbor sins,
but blessed is he who is kind to the needy.*

PROVERBS 14:21

Your neighbor is anyone God puts in your path or on your heart. Treating your neighbor kindly is more than waving to her from your car. Begin by lending a hand with your neighbor's yard work, providing a meal to a street-corner beggar, or mailing a check to a Christian world relief organization.

*Gracious God, teach my children
to be kind to their neighbors and those
in need in the community
and throughout the world. Amen.*

Love Enemies

Listen, all of you. Love your enemies.
Do good to those who hate you.

LUKE 6:27 TLB

You can't love your enemies without God's help. Implore God for a heart like his and receive from him the love he has for all people. The love God gives to you will be a powerful testimony of God's goodness to those who hate you.

Loving God, give to my children
a heart like yours that they may love
their enemies and do good
to those who hate them. Amen.

Not Proud

So do not become proud,
but stand in awe.

ROMANS 11:20 NRSV

We cannot boast or take any credit for God's gift of salvation. We are all unworthy, and yet we have received forgiveness of all our sins. Let us stand in awe of God's grace.

Protect my children from pride for all they have and do. May they stand in awe of you, Lord, and give you the glory for their rich blessings. Amen.

Spirit-Filled

Do not quench the Spirit.

1 THESSALONIANS 5:19 NRSV

A Spirit-filled life craves time with God, desires to be obedient, and eagerly tells others of Jesus. However, a Spirit-quenched life is too proud to depend on God, too busy to read the Bible, and too selfish to talk about Jesus. If you have quenched the Spirit, repent and ask God to fill you with his Holy Spirit right now.

Holy Spirit, dwell in my children's hearts and protect them from quenching you. Amen.

Meek

Blessed are the meek,
for they will inherit the earth.

MATTHEW 5:5 NRSV

We often think of meek people in
terms of being weak. However, God
blesses the meek in faith because they
understand their exceeding sinfulness and
completely depend on him. It is the meek
who are strong in Jesus and who are rewarded.

Loving God, keep my children meek
so they surrender their lives to you and
inherit the earth. Amen.

Work Hard

*Work hard and cheerfully at all you do,
just as though you were working
for the Lord and not merely for your masters.*

COLOSSIANS 3:23 TLB

You may be in a job that is not glorious or even enjoyable. If this is the case, remember you are really working for the Lord. So be cheerful because God is your real boss, and he has your future in his hands.

*Help my children, Lord, to work
hard and cheerfully as though they were
working for you and
not merely for others. Amen.*

Pure

For God wants you to be holy and pure,
and to keep clear of all sexual sin
so that each of you will
marry in holiness and honor.

1 Thessalonians 4:3-4 tlb

A God-pleasing marriage begins with sexual purity. If you entered marriage in holiness, tell your children what a blessing purity is to your marriage. If you did not, don't let your past prevent you from teaching your children what God demands.

God, put a hedge of protection
around my children so they may enter
marriage holy and pure. Amen.

Put God First

In everything you do, put God first,
and he will direct you and
crown your efforts with success.

PROVERBS 3:6 TLB

Beauty queens wear crowns, star athletes receive trophies, and successful business people accumulate wealth. Whether or not you are successful in the world's view, God has a crown for you. If you put God first in all you do and are directed by him, your efforts to serve him will be crowned with success.

Lord God, guide my children to put
you first in everything they do, direct
them in the way they should go, and
crown their efforts with success. Amen.

Alive in Christ

*I know your works; you have
a name of being alive, but you are dead.
Wake up, and strengthen what
remains and is on the point of death.*

REVELATION 3:1-2 NRSV

Your physical fitness will deteriorate
without a healthy diet and exercise.
The same is true of your spiritual fitness.
Read your Bible daily, pray unceasingly, and
worship regularly to strengthen your faith.

*Heavenly Father, wake up a desire
in my children to be spiritually fit
and alive in Christ in both
name and works. Amen.*

Committed

Commit everything you do to the Lord.
Trust him to help you do it and he will.

PSALM 37:5 TLB

During our lifetime we make numerous
commitments—to exercise regularly,
control our temper, read our Bible daily—
and all too frequently break them. We struggle
to succeed when we lean on our own power
and strength. However, if we commit
everything we do to the Lord, and trust him
to help us do it, he will give us his power
and strength to triumph.

Eternal Lord, help my children to
commit everything they do to you and
to trust you to help them do it. Amen.

Childlike Faith

Let the little children come to me!
Never send them away! For the Kingdom
of God belongs to [people] who have
hearts as trusting as these little children's.

LUKE 18:16 TLB

Children depend on adults to provide
for them and tend to their needs.
However, as they mature, they become
independent. Paradoxically, as we mature in
faith, we become totally dependent on God
and come to him as little children in total
trust that he will provide for our every need.

Jesus, sustain my children's
childlike trust in you as they mature.
Amen.

Assured Understanding

I want their hearts to be encouraged and united in love, so that they may have all the riches of assured understanding and have the knowledge of God's mystery, that is, Christ himself, in whom are hidden all the treasures of wisdom and knowledge.

COLOSSIANS 2:2-3 NRSV

You can be assured of eternal salvation if you confess your sins and put your trust in Jesus. Assurance of salvation is not the result of your efforts but because of God's grace. Give your life to Jesus and receive all the riches of assured understanding and knowledge of God's plan of salvation through Christ.

Father, give to my children full assurance of your salvation through Christ Jesus. Amen.

Control Tongue

For by your words you will be justified,
and by your words you will be condemned.

MATTHEW 12:37 NRSV

Your tongue must be controlled to avoid condemnation of yourself and the destruction of others. Keep in mind that on the Day of Judgment you will give an account of every careless word spoken. With God's help you can control your tongue and teach your children through loving words.

Holy God, direct my children
to glorify you with their words and to
control their tongues. Amen.

Responsible

*For we are each
responsible for our own conduct.*
GALATIANS 6:5 NLT

We often play the blame game by
pointing the finger at everyone but
ourselves. Our children learn the game from
us at an early age. Teach your children to
accept responsibility for their actions by
hearing you say, "I am sorry. I was wrong."

*Lord, help my children learn to be
responsible for their own conduct.
Amen.*

Belong to God

The person who belongs to God
accepts what God says.

JOHN 8:47 NCV

I f you are a Christian, you accept the whole
Bible as God's inspired Word. You do not
pick and choose pieces of God's truth and
discard the rest. Do you belong to God?

Father, may my children
belong to you and accept your Word
as truth. Amen.

Example

Set the believers an example in speech
and conduct, in love, in faith, in purity.

1 TIMOTHY 4:12 NRSV

Does your life contradict the words
spoken to your children? Are you
telling your children to trust God and yet
you show no reliance on him? What example
are you really setting for your children?

Lord Jesus, teach my children to set an
example in speech and conduct,
in love, in faith, and in purity. Amen.

Maturing in Faith

*Therefore let us leave the elementary teachings
about Christ and go on to maturity.*

HEBREWS 6:1

Your faith must mature from the
elementary teachings of "repent and
believe." It is time to grow up and have a
deeper understanding of a life with Christ.
Live out your faith by witnessing to the
unsaved, mentoring the less mature in faith,
and obediently following God's call to holiness.

*Jesus, nurture my children to mature
in their faith and to strive for
a deeper understanding of you. Amen.*

Hate Lies

*A good man hates lies; wicked men lie
constantly and come to shame.*

PROVERBS 13:5 TLB

Lies hurt others, bring shame to the liar,
and grieve God. Hate lies by requiring
and expecting your children to tell the truth.
Teach them that speaking the truth
honors God.

*Holy God, restrain my children's urge
to lie. Amen.*

Good

*And we know that in all things
God works for the good of those
who love him, who have been called
according to his purpose.*

ROMANS 8:28

Bad things happen because we live in a fallen, sinful world. However, be assured that in all things God works for your good if you love him and are heeding his call. You may not see the good now, but trust God's eternal perspective and timing.

*God, when my children run
into disappointments, assure them that
you work for the good of those
who love you and are living according
to your purpose. Amen.*

Confess With Lips

*If you confess with your lips
that Jesus is Lord and believe in your
heart that God raised him from
the dead, you will be saved.*

ROMANS 10:9 RSV

Faith is not secretive or private. Your confession takes your faith into the open to tell the world that God has rescued you from eternal hell. Tell everyone the Good News.

*Holy God, inspire my children
to confess with their lips that Jesus is
Lord and believe in their hearts
that you raised Jesus from the dead so
they will be saved. Amen.*

Listen

*This is my beloved Son, and I am
fully pleased with him. Listen to him.*

MATTHEW 17:5 NLT

Public service announcements provide an
important message to their listeners.
If God's message at Jesus' baptism were given
today it might be phrased as *Jesus is cool;
let him rule.* Are you listening?

*Almighty Lord, urge my children
to listen to your beloved Son
as they hear your Word. Amen.*

Model Good Deeds

Show yourself in all respects
a model of good deeds.

TITUS 2:7 RSV

Your children are watching you and learning how to behave. Knowing this, teach them to serve God by helping the poor, feeding the hungry, and ministering to those in need. Become their model of good deeds.

Holy God, inspire my children
to be models of good deeds to reflect the
love you have shown them through
your Son, Jesus Christ. Amen.

Cheerful Giver

*Each of you must give as you have made
up your mind, not reluctantly or under
compulsion, for God loves a cheerful giver.*

2 CORINTHIANS 9:7 NRSV

God has given you all things. In fact, he
gave his only Son to die for your sins.
How then can you not give cheerfully from
the bounty God has provided for you?

*Gracious God, motivate my children
to have an attitude of gratitude and to
be cheerful givers. Amen.*

Sow Generously

Remember this: Whoever sows sparingly
will also reap sparingly, and whoever sows
generously will also reap generously.

2 CORINTHIANS 9:6

S ome people can't understand why they
are without true friends. If you count
yourself among that group, step back and
think about the last time you helped
someone without expecting anything in
return. Remember, you reap what you sow.

Lord Jesus, help my children
understand that to have friends they
need to be a friend. Amen.

Trust

I trust in God's unfailing love
for ever and ever.

PSALM 52:8

A spouse's love may waiver, and friends may come and go, but you can always count on God's constant love.

Even when you may not feel loved, you can trust God in all circumstances at all times to be with you and love you unconditionally. His love is eternal, dependable, and perfect.

I pray, dear God,
my children will trust in your unfailing
love forever. Amen.

Image of God

*So God created human beings
in his image. In the image of God he created
them. He created them male and female.*

GENESIS 1:27 NCV

Magazine models make us question our
appearance. Children influenced by
glamour and glitz become dissatisfied with
their own features. Let your children know
that they are perfect just the way God
made them.

*Almighty God and Creator,
help my children to appreciate that you
created them in your image. Amen.*

Salt

You are the salt of the earth.

MATTHEW 5:13

You are God's salt, his seasoning and preservative. Flavor the world with the message of salvation through Jesus Christ. Preserve God's goodness in the world by the way you live your life.

Jesus, make my children the salt of the earth by telling others about the Gospel message, and keep my children close to you so they do not lose their saltiness. Amen.

Light

You are the light of the world.
MATTHEW 5:14

Too many people live in the darkness of a life without Christ. As a believer, you are to bring the light of the Gospel to others. Shine your light by speaking up about your faith, inviting a neighbor to church, and telling your children and others how God is working in your life.

Lord, may my children be a bright light in this dark world so unbelievers may see you through them. Amen.

Kind

*Be kind and loving to each other,
and forgive each other, just as God
forgave you in Christ.*

EPHESIANS 4:32 NCV

Do you ever feel like a referee in your home? Teach your children that God values kindness and requires them to be as loving and forgiving to others as he has been toward them. Kindness must be extended worldwide, but it begins at home.

*Jesus, help my children
to be kind to one another. Amen.*

Compassionate

As God's chosen ones,
holy and beloved, clothe yourselves with
compassion, kindness, humility,
meekness, and patience.

Colossians 3:12 nrsv

Jesus' compassion for God's people directed his life's work and brought him to the cross. As God's chosen one, holy and beloved, have you clothed yourself with compassion? Are you concerned for the spiritually lost, having a desire to bring them to a saving relationship with Jesus?

O God, clothe my children
in compassion, kindness, humility,
meekness, and patience. Amen.

Lean Not on Own Understanding

Trust in the Lord with all your heart and lean not on your own understanding.

PROVERBS 3:5

Most of us don't understand how airplanes or automobiles work and yet we completely trust them to work as intended. Likewise, we may not understand the workings of God and yet we fully trust him. Know that God has an eternal perspective that our human minds will never grasp.

Lord Jesus, lead my children to trust in you with all their heart and lean not on their own understanding. Amen.

Eagerly Wait

*So Christ, having been offered once
to bear the sins of many, will appear
a second time, not to deal with sin, but to
save those who are eagerly waiting for him.*

Hebrews 9:28 nrsv

Remember how your conversations and behavior overflowed with excitement for your wedding day or the birth of your child? Christians wait with eager anticipation for Christ to come again. Can others see your excitement?

*Jesus, my Savior, find my children
eagerly waiting for you
to come again on the last day.
Amen.*

Ask, Seek, Knock

Ask and it will be given you;
seek and you will find; knock and the
door will be opened to you.

MATTHEW 7:7

Unlike putting money in a vending machine, you cannot put in your prayers and get back whatever you desire. However, through prayer you can learn to crave the things of God. When your prayers are in line with God's will, you can ask and it will be given you, seek and you will find, knock and God will open the door.

Lord, help my children
come to you in prayer asking, seeking,
and knocking. Amen.

Encourager

Therefore encourage one another
and build up each other.

1 THESSALONIANS 5:11 NRSV

You are your children's number one fan in sports, music, and school activities. Are you also your children's personal cheerleader for their spiritual life? Build your children up in the faith by cheering them on in their prayer life, encouraging them to read the Bible, and supporting their fellowship with other Christians.

Heavenly Father, prompt my children
to encourage one another
and build up each other
in the faith. Amen.

Rooted in Love

*And I pray that you, being rooted
and established in love, may have power,
together with all the saints, to grasp
how wide and long and
high and deep is the love of Christ.*

EPHESIANS 3:17-18

Love allows you to catch a glimpse of
Christ's love. When you are rooted and
established in love, you have the power to
comprehend the enormity of God's love for
you. Give your children a vision of how wide
and long and high and deep is the love of
Christ for them.

*Jesus, I pray that my children
will be rooted and established in your
love and grasp how wide and long and
high and deep it is. Amen.*

Servant Leader

Whoever wants to become great
among you must serve
the rest of you like a servant.

MATTHEW 20:26 NCV

O n the night before Jesus' crucifixion, his final leadership lesson was to serve his disciples by washing their feet. Jesus demonstrated that a great leader must be willing to do the most humble job. Are you willing to do the uncelebrated job as well as the honored one?

Savior, teach my children,
as you did your disciples, that if they
want to be a leader they must
act like a servant and lead by serving
the needs of others. Amen.

Every Thought Captive

We demolish arguments and every pretension that sets itself up against the knowledge of God, and we take captive every thought to make it obedient to Christ.

2 CORINTHIANS 10:5

S atan works his way into your life through deception, distortion, and destruction of the truth. Take hold of every thought to make it obedient to Christ. Warn your children of Satan's tactics and firmly ground them in the basics of Jesus Christ.

Lord, protect my children from Satan's deception and teach them to take captive every thought to make it obedient to Christ. Amen.

Cling to Good

Hate what is evil; cling to what is good.

ROMANS 12:9

Society labels you intolerant if you take a biblical stand against some politically accepted idea. However, the Bible clearly states that some things are not good, right, or acceptable. God calls us to hate what is evil, and cling to what is good.

*Righteous God, help my children
to hate what is evil and
cling to what is good. Amen.*

Self-Controlled

*So we should not be like other people
who are sleeping, but we
should be alert and have self-control.*

1 THESSALONIANS 5:6 NCV

Teenagers have the uncanny ability
to sleep long into the day. Maybe it is
because they lack the self-control to get to
bed at an earlier hour. Don't let Jesus find
you slumbering in your faith because you
lacked the self-control to spend time with
him each day.

*Father, keep my children from
spiritual slumber; help them to be alert
and to maintain self-control. Amen.*

Call on the Lord

Anyone who calls on the Lord will be saved.

ROMANS 10:13 NCV

New mothers hear and respond to every sound their child makes. Similarly, God is ready to answer you when you call out to him. God responds with his gift of salvation to everyone who genuinely calls on his name and desires to make him first in life.

*Lord, arouse my children
to call upon your name and
be saved. Amen.*

Proclaim Christ

*For as often as you eat this bread
and drink the cup, you proclaim the
Lord's death until he comes.*

1 CORINTHIANS 11:26 NRSV

Every time we receive Holy Communion
we are proclaiming Christ's death.
Through the bread and wine we acknowledge
and praise God for sending his Son, Jesus, to
die for our sins. We also retell the story of
what Christ did for us until he comes again.

*Lord Jesus, stir up the desire within
my children to frequently come to your
table to proclaim and retell the message
of your victory over death. Amen.*

Good Steward

Like good stewards of the manifold grace of God, serve one another with whatever gift each of you has received.

1 Peter 4:10 NRSV

God has given you a spiritual gift to use in his service. Don't overlook that your gift might include driving, encouraging, organizing, fixing, cleaning, or the like. Use your gift in service to God and nurture your children's abilities to be used for God as well.

*Motivate my children, Gracious God,
to be good stewards of the
special abilities and gifts
you have given to each one. Amen.*

Show Humility

Show true humility toward all men.

TITUS 3:2

Humility comes when you understand that Christ died for you. In recognition of his sacrifice, humble yourself in service to others. Let Christ's love touch the lives of those you touch.

O Lord, grant that my children
will show true
humility toward all people.
Amen.

Meditate

*But his delight is in the law of the Lord,
and on his law he meditates day and night.*

PSALM 1:2

The Bible is God's love letter to you. Pore over that letter, meditate on his love, and dwell on his message. Delight in all that he is telling you and obediently act on what he is calling you to do.

Gracious Lord, may I pass your love letter on to my children so they too may delight in your Word and meditate on you day and night. Amen.

Know God's Will

Be joyful always; pray continually;
give thanks in all circumstances, for this
is God's will for you in Christ Jesus.

1 Thessalonians 5:16-18

Many people struggle to figure out God's will. It is really as easy as one, two, three: Be joyful, pray continually, and give thanks. Teach your children to count on God.

Lord Jesus, give my children
the understanding that your will for
them is to be joyful, prayerful,
and thankful at all times and in all
circumstances. Amen.

Attitude of Christ

*Your attitude should be
the same as that of Christ Jesus.*

PHILIPPIANS 2:5

At times we think our children need an attitude adjustment. However, our attitude probably needs a tune-up as well. Do you have an attitude the same as that of Christ Jesus?

*Jesus, bestow on my children
an attitude the same as yours. Amen.*

Bear Much Fruit

My true disciples produce much fruit.
This brings great glory to my Father.

JOHN 15:8 NLT

Y ou can identify a fruit tree by the fruit
it produces. Similarly, you can identify
those who follow Jesus by their good deeds.
Do your good deeds give evidence that you
are a Christian and bring glory to the Father?

Lord, cultivate in my children
the desire to produce much fruit
for you and so show that
they are your disciples. Amen.

Live in Harmony

Finally, all of you, live in harmony with
one another; be sympathetic, love as
brothers, be compassionate and humble.

1 PETER 3:8

Harmonious music is pleasing to the
ear. So it is when people live in
harmony. What beautiful music to God's ears
when you are more concerned about
extending sympathy, love, and compassion
than receiving it.

Jesus, my Savior, teach my children to
live in harmony with each other
by being sympathetic, loving,
compassionate, and humble. Amen.

Overflow With Love

*My prayer for you is that you will overflow
more and more with love for others,
and at the same time keep on growing in
spiritual knowledge and insight.*

PHILIPPIANS 1:9 TLB

Imagine a world where every Christian
displays God's love as easily and swiftly as
a swollen river overflows its banks. Such an
overflowing of love would wash away hatred,
prejudice, bias, and discrimination. Let God
spill over the sides of your life into your
family, neighborhood, workplace, school,
and community.

*Dear God, encourage my children to
overflow with love for others and at the
same time to keep growing in spiritual
knowledge and insight. Amen.*

Give Thanks

O give thanks to the Lord, for he is good;
for his steadfast love endures forever.

PSALM 106:1 NRSV

We frequently give thanks for food, family, and friends, but how often do we give thanks to God for his very nature and character? By doing so we are reminded of who he is and why he alone is God. When praying with your children, include thanks for God's unique attributes.

We give you thanks, O Lord,
for you are good and your steadfast love
endures forever. Amen.

Transformed

*Do not be conformed to this world,
but be transformed by the renewing of
your minds, so that you may
discern what is the will of God—what is
good and acceptable and perfect.*

ROMANS 12:2 NRSV

We are easily pressured to conform to society's values. However, God wants us to be transformed by focusing our minds on what is good, acceptable, and perfect. Begin your transformation by choosing wholesome movies, inspiring books, and worthy TV shows.

Almighty God, when my children are faced with peer pressure to do what they know is wrong, give them the strength to resist and not to conform but to be transformed to do what is good and acceptable and perfect. Amen.

Crave God's Word

Like newborn babies,
crave pure spiritual milk, so that by it
you may grow up in your salvation.

1 PETER 2:2

Christian growth requires a healthy diet of the Bread of Life found in Jesus Christ. You must feed regularly and frequently on the Word of God as well as be nourished by regular worship with fellow believers. Without spiritual nourishment, your faith will starve.

Lord Jesus, stir up a craving
in my children to study your Word
and meet with other believers
in worship so they will grow up
in their salvation. Amen.

Understand
Wages of Sin

For the wages of sin is death, but the gift of God is eternal life in Christ Jesus our Lord.

ROMANS 6:23

God cannot let sin go unpunished. Your sin, whether little or big, deserves death. Thanks be to God that he so loved the world that he gave his only Son to pay the penalty for your sins.

Christ Jesus, instill in my children the seriousness of their sin and the understanding that by grace through faith they receive forgiveness of sins. Amen.

Ears That Listen

Let anyone with ears listen!

MATTHEW 11:15 NRSV

Sometimes we are brought up short by our children's cry *You aren't listening!* When we get too busy to hear God talking to us through his Word, the Bible, or through our fellowship with other believers, God says it this way—*Let anyone with ears listen!* Have you given God your full attention today?

Lord, open my children's ears so they will listen to you. Amen.

Know God

Be still, and know that I am God.
PSALM 46:10

I ronically, we often miss out on life when we get so busy just living it. Similarly, you may be so occupied doing things for the Lord that you miss out on time alone with him. Make quiet time each day to be still and know God.

God Almighty, lead my children to find quiet times to be still and know that you are God. Amen.

Pure in Heart

Blessed are the pure in heart,
for they will see God.

MATTHEW 5:8

A pure heart is free from selfish desires and sinful passions. It is a heart like God's that is loving, compassionate, and willing to minister to the needs of others. Of course the pure in heart see God— they share his heart.

Gracious God, help my children
to be pure in heart to serve you. Amen.

Wear Whole Armor

Put on the whole armor of God,
so that you may be able to
stand against the wiles of the devil.

EPHESIANS 6:11 NRSV

The devil is real and out to conquer your soul. Jesus has already won the war, but you must fight daily temptations until he comes again. Prepare for each battle by wearing Christ's righteousness, holding the shield of faith, and wielding the Word of God.

Invincible God, clothe my children
with your armor so that they may
withstand the wiles of the devil. Amen.

Have Faith

Faith means being sure of the things
we hope for and knowing that something
is real even if we do not see it.... Without
faith no one can please God.

HEBREWS 11:1, 6 NCV

We can't see the wind, but we see its
effects. Similarly, we may not see
God face-to-face in this lifetime, but we do
see the evidence of his existence when we
look at the beauty of the world, the intricacy
of the human body, and the miracle of birth.
Faith knows something is true even if it can't
be seen.

God, give to my children
a mighty faith. Amen.

Yearn

My soul yearns, even faints,
for the courts of the Lord; my heart and
my flesh cry out for the living God.

PSALM 84:2

Our hearts yearn to be with the one we love. This ache is also present when we long to be in the presence of the Lord. Draw near to God, and he will draw near to you and satisfy that ache in your soul.

Living God, may my children's souls
yearn for you; may their
hearts cry out to you. Amen.

Clean Heart

Create in me a clean heart, O God.
Renew a right spirit within me.

PSALM 51:10 NLT

Y ou cannot erase your own sins no
matter how good you try to be.
God gives you a clean heart when you
confess your sinful desire to be in control of
your own life and be your own god.
Come now and surrender control of your life
to God, and he will renew your spirit.

Create in my children a clean heart,
O God, and renew
a right spirit within them. Amen.

Shine

In the same way, let your light shine
before others, so that they
may see your good works and give glory
to your Father in heaven.

MATTHEW 5:16 NRSV

If you love Jesus, let your conversations
and actions exemplify a life in Christ.
Take a stand for Jesus in your home,
community, and beyond. Actively share your
faith with your children and those you come
in contact with each day so glory may be
given to your Father in heaven.

Let my children's light so shine
before all people, Loving God, so that
all may see their good works and give
glory to you. Amen.

Confess Christ

So that every knee will bow to the name of Jesus—everyone, in heaven, on earth, and under the earth. And everyone will confess that Jesus Christ is Lord, and bring glory to God the Father.

PHILIPPIANS 2:10-11 NCV

When Jesus comes again every person will bow before Almighty God and confess that Jesus is Lord. Believers will once again make that confession, and unbelievers will come to the eternal realization that their confession is too late. Do not delay in leading your children to confess that Jesus is their Lord.

Jesus, lead my children to bow down and confess that you are Lord and so bring glory to God the Father. Amen.

Grow in Grace

But grow in the grace and knowledge of
our Lord and Savior Jesus Christ.

2 PETER 3:18 NCV

It is silly to expect your children to stay
infants forever. Equally ridiculous is to think
their faith should remain immature. It is your
job to feed your children with God's Word so
that they grow in the grace and knowledge of
our Lord and Savior Jesus Christ.

The seed of faith has been planted, Lord.
Help it take root and grow in the
grace and knowledge of Jesus. Amen.

Endure Testing

God is faithful, and he will not let you
be tested beyond your strength, but with
the testing he will also provide the way
out so that you may be able to endure it.

1 Corinthians 10:13 nrsv

Y ou cannot resist temptation by your
own power. During times of temptation
and testing, trust God to provide the
strength to endure and a means of escape.
Also, teach your children to turn to God in
their moments of testing.

Faithful Lord, when my children
are confronted with peer pressure
and temptations loom, show them the
way out so they may be able
to endure it. Amen.

Dependent on God

*When you bow down before the Lord
and admit your dependence on him,
he will lift you up and give you honor.*

JAMES 4:10 NLT

Wealth, family, or abilities become your god if you rely on them instead of God. The Lord is the only true living God. Recognize your dependency on him and make him Lord of your life.

Lord, open my children's eyes to their dependency on you so you may lift them up and give them honor. Amen.

Know Right From Wrong

For I want you always to see clearly the difference between right and wrong, and to be inwardly clean, no one being able to criticize you from now until our Lord returns.

PHILIPPIANS 1:10 TLB

The line between right and wrong is frequently crossed. Violence, vulgar language, and sexual themes have become so commonplace that we become numb to behavior that God clearly states is wrong. God's perfect holy ways are the standard, not society's ever-changing values.

Father, I pray that my children will always see clearly the difference between right and wrong, and that they will be inwardly clean. Amen.

Know God's Will

We have not stopped praying for you and asking God to fill you with the knowledge of his will through all spiritual wisdom and understanding…that you may live a life worthy of the Lord and may please him in every way: bearing fruit in every good work, growing in the knowledge of God.

COLOSSIANS 1:9-10

As your children grow spiritually, help them learn the discipline of studying God's Word and spending quiet time in prayer. Through your daily example, show them how to make this habit their own.

O God, fill my children with knowledge of your will for their lives that they may lead a life worthy of you and may please you in every way. Amen.

Cling to the Lord

My soul clings to you;
your right hand upholds me.

PSALM 63:8 NRSV

Frightened children cling to their
mothers for safety and assurance.
Similarly, we should be frightened of life
without God. Cling to him as if your
life depends on him, because it does.

Jesus, may my children's souls
cling to you; may your right hand
uphold them. Amen.

Silence Ignorant Talk

*For it is God's will that by
doing good you should silence the ignorant
talk of foolish men.*

1 PETER 2:15

Y ou can't argue against good. Making
godly choices and treating others well
can silence the ignorant talk of foolish people.
If you bring the Good News of Jesus Christ
to others, you will provide the reason for
your doing good and bring honor to God.

*Lord Jesus, strengthen my children's faith
when challenged by people who
resist knowing you. Help my children
to do good and thereby silence the
ignorant talk of foolish people. Amen.*

Victorious

But thanks be to God, who always leads
us in victory through Christ.

2 CORINTHIANS 2:14 NCV

I f you focus on earthly victories, you lose
sight of the more important victory
received through Jesus. His victory over sin,
death, and the devil is immeasurably and
eternally more important than any earthly
victory. Stay with God who leads you in
eternal victory through Christ.

Holy God, thanks be to you for
leading my children in victory over sin
and worldly temptations. Amen.

Trained in Godliness

Train yourself in godliness.
1 TIMOTHY 4:7 NRSV

Like a well-trained athlete, you too must be dedicated to train yourself in godliness. First, acknowledge Jesus as Lord of your life and ask God to fill you with the Holy Spirit and his power. Thereafter, diligently study God's Word and obey His truths.

*Dear Jesus, encourage my children
to train themselves in godliness
and uphold your values. Amen.*

Bold

*Let us therefore approach the throne
of grace with boldness, so that
we may receive mercy and find grace
to help in time of need.*

HEBREWS 4:16 NRSV

Jesus' death provides us direct access to
God. No longer do we need a high priest
or other saint to bring our petitions to God.
Come now, boldly and directly, pouring out
before God your praises, confessions,
thanksgivings, and requests to receive his
mercy and grace.

*Almighty God, with boldness let my
children draw near to receive
your mercy and find grace to help in
time of need. Amen.*

Test Everything

Test everything. Hold on to the good.

1 Thessalonians 5:21

Children are bombarded with different ideas and world philosophies. Train them to test every idea against what the Bible says. Teach them to hold onto biblical principles and discard the rest.

Jesus, direct my children to know your Word so they may test everything and hold on to the good. Amen.

Useful to Christ

*If any one purifies himself from what
is ignoble, then he will be a vessel for noble
use, consecrated and useful to the master of
the house, ready for any good work.*

2 Timothy 2:21 rsv

Are you ready for Jesus? Have you repented
of your sins? Have you asked Christ
how you can be useful?

*Lord, lead my children to repentance
and to prepare themselves for useful
service to you. Amen.*

Clear Conscience

*Always be prepared to give an answer
to everyone who asks you to give the
reason for the hope that you have.
But do this with gentleness
and respect, keeping a clear conscience.*

1 PETER 3:15-16

It is important to share your faith, but it must be done in love. Sometimes nonbelievers are turned away from Christianity not because of the message, but the messenger. Treat others with gentleness and respect, keeping your conscience clear, so that the presentation of the Gospel message will not only be heard but welcomed.

*Holy Lord, keep my children's consciences
clear so when they are ridiculed
for their faith they may stand secure in
their hope in you. Amen.*

Declare God's Glory

Declare his glory among the nations,
his marvelous deeds among all the peoples.

PSALM 96:3

When you receive great news, the first
thing you want to do is tell someone.
So it should be with the life-changing news
that Jesus died to save the world from sin
and hell. What are you waiting for? Declare
Jesus' marvelous deeds among all people,
especially your children.

Living Lord, help my children
declare your glory among
the nations and your marvelous deeds
among all people. Amen.

Confident

*For the Lord will be your confidence
and will keep your foot from being snared.*

PROVERBS 3:26

Life is uncertain because you don't know
what the future will bring. Nevertheless,
you can approach each day without fear
because your confidence is in the Lord.
Your salvation is secure.

*Dear God, we can trust you
to give us sure footing.
Help my children to put their confidence
in you alone. Amen.*

Abide in Christ

And now, little children, abide in him,
so that when he is revealed we may
have confidence and not be put to shame
before him at his coming.

1 JOHN 2:28 NRSV

Abide in Christ today. Surrender your life to Christ, rest in his Word, cling to him in prayer, reach out to him through serving others, and be available to answer his call. Have confidence that you will be ready when Jesus comes again.

Loving Jesus, guide my children
to abide in you so that when you come
again they may stand confidently
and say, "Here I am, Lord!
I'm ready for you!" Amen.

Know Truth

If you continue in my word, you are truly
my disciples; and you will know
the truth, and the truth will make you free.

JOHN 8:31-32 NRSV

How do you figure out what is true in today's sea of information and claims of truth? If information or societal ideas conflict with biblical truths, then hold fast to what the Bible teaches. Do not change the teachings of the Bible to fit society; change society to fit the Bible.

Lord Jesus, with so much confusion in
this world, help my children to learn
what is true by studying your Word and
living according to your truth. Amen.

Justified

Therefore, since we are justified by faith,
we have peace with God
through our Lord Jesus Christ.

ROMANS 5:1 NRSV

God has repaired your broken relationship
with him. Through faith in Jesus'
atonement on the cross, your sins are
forgiven and you are justified through faith.
Oh, what peace you experience when you are
no longer an enemy of God!

Bless my children, Father God,
with the peace of justification received
through faith in Jesus Christ. Amen.

Safe

If you trust in the Lord, you will be safe.

PROVERBS 29:25 NCV

When your children are afraid, they come to you knowing they are safe. Do they also know they can go to their heavenly Father to be safe from earthly worries, sin, and death? Teach your children to put their trust in God and be eternally safe.

Almighty God, assure my children that if they trust in you, they will be safe. Amen.

Temple of the Holy Spirit

*Do you not know that your body
is a temple of the Holy Spirit, who is in
you, whom you have received from God?
You are not your own.*

1 CORINTHIANS 6:19

You should treat something very carefully when it is not yours. Your body is not your own; it is a temple of the Holy Spirit. How are you treating it?

*Holy Spirit, help my children
treat their bodies as a temple for you,
your holy dwelling place. Amen.*

Pursue Righteousness

*But you, man of God, flee from all this,
and pursue righteousness, godliness, faith,
love, endurance and gentleness.*

1 TIMOTHY 6:11

Unholy living is easy because sinning is in our nature. However, we are called to flee sin and pursue righteousness. Give your children the Bible that provides directions for which way to run.

*Holy God, give my children your
direction that they will flee
from all sin and pursue righteousness,
godliness, faith, love, endurance,
and gentleness. Amen.*

Life

*God has given us eternal life, and this life
is in his Son. He who has the Son
has life; he who does not have
the Son of God does not have life.*

1 JOHN 5:11-12

Life without faith is no life at all. If you
really intend for your children to have
life, eternal life, you must introduce them to
Jesus. Thereafter, encourage them to live life
for Jesus.

*Living God, guide my children
to believe in your Son so they may have
eternal life. Amen.*

Stand in the Gap

*I looked in vain for anyone who
would build again the wall of
righteousness that guards the land,
who could stand in the gap
and defend you from my just attacks,
but I found not one.*

Ezekiel 22:30 TLB

When was the last time you took a stand for righteousness? Have you been on your knees petitioning God on behalf of another? Do you stand in the gap, pleading with God for your children's righteousness and salvation?

*Lord, teach my children to stand
in the gap for those in need. Amen.*

Praise

Let everything that has breath praise the Lord.

PSALM 150:6

No matter your circumstances, you can praise God for who he is and his everlasting love for you. He is the Creator of the universe, the Redeemer of your soul, and the Life in your life. How awesome is God.

May my children burst forth in praise to you, Almighty and Everlasting God. Amen.

Strength in God

God is our refuge and strength,
a very present help in trouble.

PSALM 46:1 NRSV

Where do you seek refuge in times of trouble? Do you go to God for help and strength or take refuge in friends, love, alcohol, or drugs? Nothing is too hard for God, so bring your troubles to him and be strengthened.

Create a desire in my children
to seek you first, Lord, when troubles come.
Be my children's
refuge and strength. Amen.

New Creation

So if anyone is in Christ, there is a new creation: everything old has passed away; see, everything has become new!

2 Corinthians 5:17 nrsv

You are a new creation when you repent and put your trust in Christ. Worldly pleasures bring discomfort as you live in obedience to the Lord. Everything becomes new, including your movie picks, book selections, TV preferences, and language choices.

Make my children a new creation in you, O Lord. Amen.

Receive Outcome of Faith

Although you have not seen him,
you love him; and even though you do not
see him now, you believe in him and
rejoice with an indescribable and glorious joy,
for you are receiving the outcome of your
faith, the salvation of your souls.

1 PETER 1:8-9 NRSV

We teach our children that for every choice there is a consequence. There is also an eternal consequence of accepting or rejecting Christ—heaven or hell. Are you teaching your children the importance of receiving Christ?

Thank you, God, for the promise that
the outcome of our faith is the salvation
of our souls. May my children praise you
for their faith and salvation. Amen.

Accept Others

*Christ accepted you so you should accept
each other, which will bring glory to God.*

ROMANS 15:7 NCV

C hrist died for you while you were still
a sinner. With a grateful heart, you
too accept others with all their faults and
differences. Begin by accepting your children
as God made them so they learn to accept
others who may be different from them.

*Through your example, Jesus,
teach my children to accept and welcome
others in Christian love
no matter their differences.
Amen.*

Endure

By your endurance you will gain your souls.

LUKE 21:19 NRSV

God does not promise an easy life because you believe in him. Jesus said you will have troubles; yet hold firmly to the faith and live obediently. Surrender your life to Jesus to receive the strength to endure this temporal life and know the salvation of your soul.

*Jesus, when my children are teased and persecuted for their faith,
help them to know that by their endurance through you they will have assurance of salvation. Amen.*

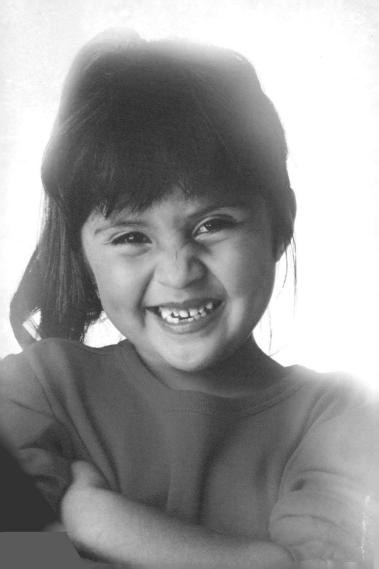

Not Condemned

Therefore, there is now no condemnation for those who are in Christ Jesus.

ROMANS 8:1

By grace you have been saved, through faith in Jesus, who paid the penalty for your sins. God does not condemn you if you are in Christ Jesus and have committed your life to him. If you have not made Christ the center of your life, now is the time to repent and put your trust in him.

Gracious Lord, bring my children to faith in you and to experience the joy of knowing there is now no condemnation for them who are in Christ Jesus. Amen.

Rejoice

Rejoice in the Lord always;
again I will say, Rejoice.

PHILIPPIANS 4:4 NRSV

Sometimes our everyday worries consume our lives. We lose sight of the big picture—that God has forgiven all our sins. Take a moment to tell God what is on your mind and rejoice in the Lord for his eternal blessings.

❋

Lord, inspire my children to come to you in prayer and to rejoice. Amen.

Seek God

But seek first his kingdom and his righteousness, and all these things will be given to you as well.

Matthew 6:33

What are your priorities? Do you seek money, success, or love more than God? What do your children see as your top priority?

Lord God, guide my children to seek first your kingdom and to obediently serve you. Amen.

Perfect

Be perfect, therefore,
as your heavenly Father is perfect.

MATTHEW 5:48 NRSV

Until you give your life to Jesus you will
never be perfect as your heavenly
Father is perfect. Confess your sins and tell
God today that your life is his. Trust him to
cleanse you from all unrighteousness and
make your life perfect in Christ.

Heavenly Father, we come to you
unworthy and seek your forgiveness.
Thank you for making my children perfect
through your Son, Jesus Christ. Amen.

Mustard Seed Faith

I tell you the truth, if you have faith
as small as a mustard seed. . . .
Nothing will be impossible for you.

MATTHEW 17:20

Even a mustard seed faith has potential to grow greatly. Nourish that seed of faith by joining a Bible study or small group, surround yourself with mature Christian mentors, and come to God in prayer. As your relationship with God blossoms, pass your spiritual enthusiasm on to your children.

Jesus, my Savior, give to my children
a mustard seed faith that will
grow into greatness for you. Amen.

Sanctified

May God himself, the God of peace,
sanctify you through and through.

<small>1 Thessalonians 5:23</small>

G od himself has set you apart for his
sacred purpose. You are not like
unbelievers without a focus. So don't act
like it.

God, sanctify my children
for your sacred purpose.
Steer my children in your ways
to fulfill your will. Amen.

Treasured Possession

For you are a people holy to the Lord
your God. Out of all the peoples on the
face of the earth, the Lord has
chosen you to be his treasured possession.

DEUTERONOMY 14:2

Your children are precious. Moreover,
they are God's treasured possession.
Be sure they know it by telling them each day.

Lord, help me to tell my children each
day how much I love them and that
they are your treasured possession, loved
with an everlasting love. Amen.

Understand God's Will

Therefore do not be foolish,
but understand what the Lord's will is.

EPHESIANS 5:17

The Bible is God's inspired, inerrant, infallible Word, providing answers to all life's important questions. However, a Bible accessorizing a coffee table doesn't help unless you read, study, and pray over God's message to you. Only a fool would have God's directions and not read them.

O Lord, keep my children
from foolishness. Inspire them
to read your Word so they
understand your will. Amen.

Live and Die
in Christ

For to me, living is Christ, and dying is gain.
PHILIPPIANS 1:21 NRSV

Living for Christ brings glory to God; dying
in Christ ushers us into an eternity
with Him. In both life and death we can
honor our Lord.

*Righteous Jesus, help my children
understand that to live
gives them opportunities for serving you
and to die brings them
into your presence forever. Amen.*

Knowledgeable

The fear of the Lord
is the beginning of knowledge.

PROVERBS 1:7

The beginning of knowledge only starts once you understand who God is and gain a reverent fear of him. After that, all life experiences are put in their proper perspective. You begin to comprehend the enormity of your sins and your need for forgiveness offered through Christ.

All-Knowing God, grant to
my children a profound
reverence for you.
Amen.

See Glory

The heavens are telling
the glory of God; and the firmament
proclaims his handiwork.

PSALM 19:1 NRSV

I f the heavens and earth are shouting out
about the glory of God, shouldn't you too?
Proclaim the Good News of Jesus. Tell your
children how you have experienced God
today in creation, during your quiet time in
prayer, or while reading the Scriptures.

Creator God, when my children
observe your creation all around them
may they contemplate your
glory and give thanks to you. Amen.

Keep the Faith

*I have fought the good fight, I have
finished the race, I have kept the faith.*

2 TIMOTHY 4:7

What do you do when unbelievers or
doubts challenge your faith? Do you
shrink back or hang tough? Fight the good
fight by using God's Word to help you answer
others and assail your personal doubts.

✻

*Faithful God, at the end of my children's
lives, may they be able to say,
"I have fought the good fight,
I have finished the race,
I have kept the faith." Amen.*

Ready

Therefore you also must be ready, for the Son of Man is coming at an unexpected hour.

MATTHEW 24:44 NRSV

Mothers are frequently getting their children ready for some event. Have you prepared your children to meet Jesus? Do they know him personally?

Jesus, keep my children ever ready to meet you face-to-face. Amen.

Hunger and Thirst for Righteousness

*Blessed are those who hunger and thirst
for righteousness, for they will be filled.*

MATTHEW 5:6

Your children need a healthy diet of
God. Are you serving them daily
portions of God's Word, dishing out the fruit
of the Spirit, and filling their plate with
ministry opportunities? Remember to feed
your children's souls or they will starve.

*God, give to my children
a true hunger for your Word and let
them be filled. Amen.*

Judge Not

Do not judge,
so that you may not be judged.

MATTHEW 7:1 NRSV

Too often we judge others by their
appearance, bank account, address,
or education. But God alone knows what is
in the heart. Do not let your judgments
prevent others from seeing God's love in you
and for them.

Lord, help my children to recognize
their own sin rather than
judging the sins of others. Amen.

Suffer for God

They…[rejoiced] that God had counted them worthy to suffer dishonor for his name.

ACTS 5:41 TLB

W hy are you afraid to talk about your faith? Are you afraid of being teased, harassed, or even persecuted? Ironically, when you suffer for Christ you can rejoice that God has counted you worthy to suffer for his name's sake.

May my children rejoice in the honor to suffer for you, Holy God. Amen.

Pure Mind

Set your minds on things above,
not on earthly things.

COLOSSIANS 3:2

The world is vying to fill your mind
with ungodly information and images.
The choices you make and the examples
you set either support worldly values or
God's values. Fill your mind with God-
centered thoughts and keep it focused on
things above.

Holy Lord, help my children
to focus on things with a heavenly value,
not on things of earthly value. Amen.

Just

The Lord is just in all his ways,
and kind in all his doings.

PSALM 145:17 NRSV

God's justice is perfect—from the past
to the present and the future.
We may not always agree how his justice is
administered, but then we don't have God's
eternal perspective. Whose justice are you
going to trust?

Righteous God, help my children to be
just and kind in all they do. Amen.

Share Faith

*I pray that you may be active
in sharing your faith, so that you will
have a full understanding of every good
thing we have in Christ.*

PHILEMON 1:6

We teach our children to share their
toys. Do we also teach them to share
their faith? If children learned to share the
Gospel while learning to share their toys,
each generation would easily tell others
of Jesus.

*Christ Jesus, I pray that my children
may be active in sharing their faith
and come to understand all the good
that is theirs in you. Amen.*

Examined

Let us test and examine our ways,
and return to the Lord!

LAMENTATIONS 3:40 RSV

Products are often tested under stressful conditions to ensure they hold up and perform as required. Similarly, you need to test and examine your ways to see if they are God's ways. Examine yourself for weakness and return to God for spiritual strength.

Merciful God, move my children
to test and examine their ways
so that if they have strayed they
may return to you. Amen.

Inspired

All scripture is inspired by God
and profitable for teaching, for reproof,
for correction, and for training in
righteousness, that the [people] of God may
be complete, equipped for every good work.

2 TIMOTHY 3:16 RSV

The Bible is God's recipe for a taste of
the heaven-bound life. His directions are
flawless and provide all you need for teaching,
disciplining, correcting, and training for every
good work. Are you following God's perfect
directions or creating your own potluck?

God, help my children to grasp
that the words of the Bible come from
you as you inspired people to write down
your will so that they can know your
truths for life. Amen.

Heaven Focused

When I look at your heavens,
the work of your fingers, the moon and
the stars that you have established; what
are human beings that you are mindful of
them, mortals that you care for them?

PSALM 8:3-4 NRSV

The vastness of the universe is mind-boggling. How great is our God who created such wonders and yet is mindful of our need for Jesus. Be reminded of God's great love for you every time you look up into the night sky.

Heavenly Father, when my children see
the majesty of your universe may they
praise you that you are mindful of them
and care for them. Amen.

Heart and Soul
for God

*Love the Lord your God with
all your heart, all your soul, all your
strength, and all your mind.*

LUKE 10:27 NCV

Love God with your whole being. Love him with all your heart by loving others; love him with all your soul by bringing the Gospel to the unsaved; love him with all your strength by lending a helping hand to those in need; and love him with all your mind by seeking his will through prayer and Bible study.

*Mighty Lord, I pray that my children
will love you with all of their heart,
soul, strength, and mind. Amen.*

Stand Mature

*Stand mature and fully assured
in all the will of God.*

COLOSSIANS 4:12 RSV

Life can be uncertain. However, you can
be fully assured that everything in
God's will is perfect. Grow in faith through
Bible study, obedience, and prayer so that
you may stand mature and fully assured of
your salvation.

*Help my children to stand mature
and fully assured in your will,
O God. Amen.*

Sufficient Grace

My grace is sufficient for you,
for my power is made perfect in weakness.

2 CORINTHIANS 12:9

S ometimes God puts obstacles in your
path to catch your attention. In your
times of powerlessness, you finally hear God
plainly: "My grace is sufficient for you."
God's power is made perfect in your weakness
as you depend on him.

Draw my children close to you, God,
when they hear you say,
"My grace is sufficient." Help them
to understand that your power is made
perfect in their weakness. Amen.

Loving

We love, because he first loved us.

1 JOHN 4:19

Children first learn about love in the home. As a Christian parent, model the love God has shown you. Abundantly love your children whether or not such love is welcomed or returned.

*Dear Father, we love others
because you first loved us.
Help my children to understand the
depth of your love. Amen.*

Led by the Spirit

*For all who are led by the Spirit of God
are children of God.*

ROMANS 8:14 NLT

Are you a self-reliant, take-charge kind of person? Have you been ignoring God or pushing him to the sidelines? If so, it is time to let God take the lead.

*Holy Spirit, lead my children
and help them to let go of their own
selfish ambitions and desires. Amen.*

Submit to God

Submit yourselves therefore to God.
Resist the devil, and he will flee from you.

JAMES 4:7 NRSV

Selfishness is from the devil; selflessness is from God. Resist the devil by surrendering your self to God. Tell God you are powerless without him and want him to take charge of every aspect of your life.

Almighty God, create in my children
a desire to submit to you and
to resist the devil by surrendering their
lives to you. Amen.

Treasure in Heaven

Do not store up for yourselves treasures on earth...but store up for yourselves treasures in heaven.... For where your treasure is, there your heart will be also.

MATTHEW 6:19-21 NRSV

Yard sales are reminders that today's earthly treasures are tomorrow's discards. Keep your heart heaven bound. Donate the money you want to spend on another pair of shoes or household gadget to someone who really needs it.

Precious Jesus, as the materialism of this world contends for my children's attention, grant them strength to focus on storing up treasures in heaven. Amen.

Earnest

Those whom I love I rebuke and discipline. So be earnest, and repent.

REVELATION 3:19

Are you sometimes more sorry for getting caught than for the wrong done? God sees all, even the sins committed in secret, and he desires that you earnestly repent of your sins, not for being caught. You have sinned against a holy God, so come now with great sorrow and repent.

Lord God, thank you for loving my children so much that you rebuke and discipline them. Bring them to earnest repentance of their sins. Amen.

Even Tempered

*A man of knowledge uses words
with restraint, and a man of
understanding is even-tempered.*

PROVERBS 17:27

Is your temper causing your children
anxiety? A quick temper is unpredictable
and frightens children. Seek God's help to
use restraint and become even tempered.

*Beloved God, keep me even tempered
so my children learn from me
to use words with restraint and to manage
their temper in a godly way. Amen.*

Guard Tongue

He who guards his mouth and his tongue
keeps himself from calamity.

PROVERBS 21:23

Words are powerful. They easily lift up or tear down. Guard your tongue and stay out of trouble.

Eternal Lord, guard
my children's tongues from spewing out
hurtful words. Amen.

Act Justly

And what does the Lord require of you?
To act justly and to love mercy and to
walk humbly with your God.

MICAH 6:8

Like teenagers, we sometimes cry out to
God and say, "What do you want
from me?" God has provided a clear answer.
Treat others fairly, be forgiving, and walk
obediently with him.

Faithful God, help my children
to act justly, love mercy, and walk
humbly with you. Amen.

Flee Youthful Desires

Flee the evil desires of youth,
and pursue righteousness, faith, love and
peace, along with those who call on the
Lord out of a pure heart.

2 TIMOTHY 2:22

The evil desires of youth are powerful because "everyone is doing it." Equip your children to know God's standards and encourage right living. Counsel them to run to God in prayer, imploring him for help to pursue righteousness, faith, love, peace, and friends who share their faith.

Invincible God, guard my children from the evil desires of youth, and help them pursue righteousness, faith, love, and peace, along with those who call on the Lord out of a pure heart. Amen.

Hear and Listen

Hear the word of the Lord....
Listen to the teaching of our God.

ISAIAH 1:10 NRSV

Do you hear God speaking to you
through his Word and fellowship with
other believers? Are you listening to his
teachings through regular worship in church
and participation in small group Bible studies?
Maybe it's time to pay attention to your Father.

Father God, open my children's ears
to hear your Word and
to listen to your teachings. Amen.

Desire Spiritual Gifts

And in any event,
you should desire the most helpful gifts.

1 Corinthians 12:31 nlt

We each have our own spiritual gifts. Do not make your children into something they are not. Desire for your children the development of their unique abilities to be used to the glory of God and the advancement of his kingdom.

Loving Father, we know that by your grace we each have a spiritual gift. Motivate my children to use their God-given talents in ministry for you. Amen.

Live on God's Word

*Jesus answered, "It is written: Man does
not live by bread alone, but on every
word that comes from the mouth of God."*

MATTHEW 4:4

Your diet is not complete if it only
includes physical nourishment.
Your spiritual body must also be fed with the
Word of God through daily Bible study. Share
Jesus, the Bread of Life, with your children.

*Jesus, may my children
crave your Word every day.
Amen.*

Mind of Christ

But we have the mind of Christ.

1 CORINTHIANS 2:16

Y ou begin to think like Christ when
you yield your life to him. Your thoughts
focus on pleasing God instead of pleasing
yourself. Your earthly pursuit is to be
obedient to God and to bring him glory.

Lord, give my children
the mind of Christ so they may live
obediently for you. Amen.

Vigorous
in the Truth

See that you go on growing in the Lord,
and become strong and
vigorous in the truth you were taught.

COLOSSIANS 2:7 TLB

Your children will not be vigorous in
the truth unless you teach them.
You must not only plant the seed of faith but
water it as well. Cultivate a desire in your
children to be strong and vigorous in the
biblical truths they are taught.

Heavenly Father, keep my children
growing in their faith, and help them to
become strong and vigorous in the
truth they were taught. Amen.

Walk in Obedience

And this is love: that we
walk in obedience to his commands.

2 JOHN 6

Knowing what you should do is one thing. Actually doing it is another. You know you should obey God, but do you?

Holy Lord, guide my children
to walk in obedience to your ways.
Amen.

Live by the Spirit

So I say, live by the Spirit, and you will not gratify the desires of the sinful nature.

Galatians 5:16

Like an addict, we crave to fulfill the desires of our sinful nature. How do we stop? Come to the foot of the cross, confessing your helplessness to change, and seek God's help to live by the Spirit.

Mighty Lord, spur my children
to live by the Spirit so they will not gratify
the desires of their sinful nature. Amen.

Blessed

*Blessed is the man who does not walk in
the counsel of the wicked or stand in the
way of sinners or sit in the seat of mockers.*

Psalm 1:1

Your friends influence your children.
Are your friends fellow believers?
Are you providing a godly example as to how
to choose friends?

*Lord God, protect my children
from walking in the counsel
of the wicked or standing
in the way of sinners or sitting in
the seat of mockers. Amen.*

Fishers of Men

"Come, follow me," Jesus said,
"and I will make you fishers of men."

MARK 1:17

Fishers of men are people willing to reel in souls for Christ. Follow Jesus and he will equip you with what you need for the job. Reel in your children for Christ, and teach them how to fish as well.

Jesus, energize my children to follow you and to bring others to a saving knowledge of Jesus Christ.
Make them fishers of people. Amen.

Giving

Give to everyone who asks you,
and if anyone takes what belongs to you,
do not demand it back.

LUKE 6:30

God gave us his Son to save us from sin. We do not deserve such grace, yet God freely gives. Remember, you can never out give God.

Gracious God, create in my children
a heart to give to all in need—
even before they ask. Amen.

Jesus' Friend

I have called you friends,
for everything that I learned from my
Father I have made known to you.

JOHN 15:15

Many children long to have one special
friend with whom to share secrets.
No matter the number of friends, remind
your children that Jesus is their best friend.
Jesus has shared all that the Father has made
known to him and is waiting for you to share
your life with him.

Beloved Jesus, be my children's
best friend and give them godly wisdom.
Amen.

Selfless

*Do nothing out of selfish ambition or
vain conceit, but in humility consider
others better than yourselves.*

PHILIPPIANS 2:3

We praise our children endlessly and
provide for them abundantly. As a
result, there often is a sense of entitlement
and selfish ambition. Remind your children
that selfishness dishonors God, but humility
glorifies him.

*Lord, help my children do nothing
out of selfish ambition or vain conceit,
but in humility consider
others better than themselves. Amen.*

Do Good

*May you always be doing those good,
kind things which show that you are a
child of God, for this will bring much
praise and glory to the Lord.*

PHILIPPIANS 1:11 TLB

Y ou cannot do good deeds to make
God love you more. God cannot love
you any more than he already does because
he loves you fully and completely now. Your
good deeds, however, are in thankful response
to his grace, showing that you are a child of
God desiring to bring him glory.

*Holy Father, help my children to do
those good, kind things that show
they are your children and thereby bring
praise and glory to you. Amen.*

Child of God

*We know that we are children of God
and that all the rest of the world around
us is under Satan's power and control.*

1 JOHN 5:19 TLB

What assurance you have knowing
you are a child of God! Evil may be
pressing you from every side, but your
heavenly Father will not leave you alone.
God is more powerful than Satan.

*Heavenly Father, protect my children
from the evils of this world,
and give them the assurance that they
are your children. Amen.*

Deny Self

*Then Jesus said to his disciples,
"If anyone would come after me,
he must deny himself and take up
his cross and follow me."*

MATTHEW 16:24

There is a cost to following Jesus.
You must abandon all selfish desires,
carry whatever burden God sees fit for you
to bear, and obediently follow Jesus.
Your eternal reward is worth the cost.

*Redeemer Lord, guide my children
to follow you by denying themselves and
taking up their cross.
Help them to see the eternal reward
awaiting them. Amen.*

Eager to Serve

Feed the flock of God; care for it willingly, not grudgingly; not for what you will get out of it, but because you are eager to serve the Lord.

1 Peter 5:2 tlb

People eager to serve others have learned the lesson that it is more blessed to give than to receive. Taking care of God's people brings great joy when it is done willingly and with eagerness to serve God. Do your children know the joy of serving the Lord by caring for others?

Lord, create in my children an eagerness to serve you with a willing heart by caring for your flock. Amen.

Heir to Eternal Life

So that, having been justified
by his grace, we might become heirs
having the hope of eternal life.

TITUS 3:7

We are in line for a grand inheritance. Not silver and gold, but eternal life. As believers, let your children know what they will inherit through faith in Jesus.

Gracious God, let my children
know that whether or not they receive
worldly treasures, that having
been justified by your grace they will
inherit eternal life. Amen.

Do Everything in God's Name

And whatever you do, in word or deed,
do everything in the name
of the Lord Jesus, giving thanks to God
the Father through him.

COLOSSIANS 3:17 NRSV

Jesus died for you because he loved you more than you can comprehend. This perfect love should be your motivation to serve Jesus and do everything, in word or deed, in his name. Let your conduct be in grateful response to Jesus' sacrificial love for you.

Lord Jesus, in everything my children do,
help them bring honor
to your name and gratefully serve you
in word and deed. Amen.

Called to
Eternal Life

Fight the good fight of the faith;
take hold of the eternal life,
to which you were called and for which
you made the good confession in the
presence of many witnesses.

1 TIMOTHY 6:12 NRSV

Are you afraid of death? If you have put your trust in Jesus Christ, then death has no power over you. Take hold of the eternal life to which you were called the moment you gave your life to Jesus.

Jesus, guide my children to confess
that you are their Redeemer and
to take hold of the eternal life given
through your grace. Amen.

Crucified With Christ

I have been crucified with Christ and I no longer live, but Christ lives in me.

GALATIANS 2:20

Because Jesus died for your sins, you no longer live for yourselves but for God. Christ has taken up residency within you. Make room for him.

Savior, show my children that they have been crucified with you and that you want to come into their lives; let them make room for you. Amen.

Draw Near to God

Draw near to God and
he will draw near to you.

JAMES 4:8 RSV

When a small child is hurting, we rush in to help. However, older children must draw near before we can provide comfort. So it is with our heavenly Father, who waits for his hurting children to come into his open arms.

Heavenly Father, encourage my children
to draw near to you,
knowing you are ready to comfort and
to draw them close. Amen.

Called to Belong

*And you also are among those who are
called to belong to Jesus Christ.*

ROMANS 1:6

Children struggle to belong. Many
make bad choices just to be accepted.
Assure your children that they have been
called by God, accepted exactly the way
they are, and belong to Jesus Christ.

*Lord, assure my children that
you have called them by name to belong
to Jesus Christ. Amen.*

Prepared

*Always be prepared to give an answer to
everyone who asks you to give the reason
for the hope that you have.*

1 PETER 3:15

Many people have a recurring dream
of being unprepared for a test and
wake up anxious and nervous. Do not be
unprepared for the probing questions of
unbelievers. In preparation to answer boldly,
study the Bible, commit to memory God's
Word, and pray for wisdom.

*Holy God, I pray that my children
will have a rock solid foundation
in your Word so they are prepared to
share their faith with
those who question them. Amen.*

Directed

*May the Lord direct your hearts
to the love of God and
to the steadfastness of Christ.*

2 Thessalonians 3:5 nrsv

A car's cruise control directs the car's speed to be steady whether going up hills or down. When God directs your life, you have assurance that God's love will be constant whether you're traveling up hills of trouble or down hills of despair. Let God direct your heart to his love and to the steadfastness of Christ.

*Lord God, direct my children's hearts
to your love and to an unwavering
faith in Christ. Amen.*

Shielded by God's Power

Who through faith [you] are shielded
by God's power until the coming
of the salvation that is ready
to be revealed in the last time.

1 PETER 1:5

It is time to seek shelter when rain clouds threaten. You are not shielded from the storm until you go through the door. Similarly, faith is the door, and when through faith you go to Jesus you are shielded by God's power and safe in God's hands.

All-Powerful God,
shield my children from evil until
you come again. Amen.

Undivided Heart

*Teach me your way, O Lord, and I will
walk in your truth; give me an
undivided heart, that I may fear your name.*

PSALM 86:11

We are to love God with our whole
heart. Do not divide your love for
God with some earthly pursuit or desire.
With God, it is all or nothing.

*Loving Lord, give my children an
undivided heart that they may fear your
name and walk in your truth. Amen.*

Living Sacrifice

In view of God's mercy...
offer your bodies as living sacrifices,
holy and pleasing to God.

ROMANS 12:1

Being a living sacrifice is not dying for
Christ, but with him. As a living sacrifice,
offer to Christ what he first gave to you—
your time, talents, and possessions. Lend a
helping hand, use your skills to advance the
kingdom of God, and contribute financially
to Christian causes.

Jesus, I offer my children to you
to be used in your service.
May their lives be found holy and
pleasing to you. Amen.

Fellow Citizen

Consequently, you are no longer
foreigners and aliens,
but fellow citizens with God's people
and members of God's household.

EPHESIANS 2:19

Children worry about being excluded or not picked for a team. God has chosen everyone who believes in him as a fellow citizen and a member of his household. So assure your children that they are part of the most important team, God's team.

Thank you, God, that my children
are a part of your family and members
of your household. Amen.

Strengthened Heart

Strengthen your hearts,
for the coming of the Lord is near.

JAMES 5:8 NRSV

I t is easier to endure when the end is in
sight. So it is with our faith, knowing
each day we get closer to meeting Jesus,
either at death or on the last day.
So strengthen your heart, the end is near!

Almighty God, strengthen my children's
hearts and keep them firmly
in the faith until you come again. Amen.

Pray for Life

I love the Lord because he hears my
prayers and answers them.
Because he bends down and listens,
I will pray as long as I breathe!

PSALM 116:1-2 TLB

What a beautiful picture of God bending down to hear your prayers and answer them. How wonderful to teach your children to love a living God who listens to each prayer. What a privilege to pray as long as you have breath!

Heavenly Father, thank you for hearing
and answering my prayers. Help my
children recognize the privilege to pray
as long as they have breath. Amen.

About the Author

NANCY ANN YAEGER is a mother of three, wife, homemaker, attorney, and writer. She is the Minnesota Prayer Coordinator for Moms In Touch International (MITI) and publishes a weekly prayer newsletter for the Minnesota leaders and members of MITI. Nancy Ann spends her free time on the sidelines cheering on her children playing sports, jet skiing, and watching movies with her husband in their home in Minnesota.

Acknowledgments

A huge thank-you goes to Jonathan Morrow and his mother, Deanna, who were faithful in their calling to pray. I would also like to thank those along the way who contributed to this book: my new friends at Bethany House, including Steve Oates, who recognized the merit of simple prayers, Kyle Duncan, who shared my vision, and Julie Smith, who kept me on the right path; my mom and dad who believed in me; my Moms In Touch sisters who continually lifted me up in prayer; Terry, who rescued seventy pages from the depths of my computer; Julie, Chris, Brenda, Cathy, and Jodi, who kept me in their prayers; many family and friends who encouraged me; and, especially my husband, Greg, who loved and laughed with me, and my children, Daniel, Allison, and Paul, whom I love more than life itself.

Godly Character
and Virtues Index

300

Scripture Index